Port[rait of]
a City Father

BY MICHAEL HOLLOWAY

Sheffield Hallam University

Portraits of a City Father

Published by Sheffield Hallam University Publicity and Public Relations

*B*ill Owen's most significant contribution to Sheffield was that he kept the trade union movement and the Labour Party together. Among other things this allowed the Labour Party to keep control of the City Council without dreadful in-fighting, and he sustained it over a very long period.

He created a stability which allowed long term planning and progress to be made across the city. That's a remarkable achievement and I don't know any other individual who could have done it. He wouldn't have been able to achieve what he did in further and higher education unless we'd had that sort of stability.

Mike Bower
Leader of Sheffield City Council

Portraits of a City Father

Contents

Introduction

Bill Owen was a reticent man. Lord Mayor of Sheffield, Freeman of the City, Chairman of Sheffield City Polytechnic's governing body, Justice of the Peace, President of Sheffield Trades and Labour Council, and district secretary of one of the largest and most powerful trade unions in the country, he was not slow to accept public office or public responsibility. But he disliked talking about himself.

Interviewed by a journalist a few months before his death, he turned away questions about his birth and early years in Walkley, preferring to talk about Sheffield, friends and colleagues, trade unionism and education. Newspapers searching their cuttings files for personal idiosyncrasy or public sensation to spice their obituaries when he died in September 1992 had a lean time of it.

Yet he was a key figure in the three or four decades after the second world war when Sheffield spoke affectionately of its aldermen and councillors as the City Fathers. He was a council member and a committee chairman when cradle to grave municipalism ensured that local affairs were run as benevolently and efficiently as the electorate could reasonably expect from generally well-intentioned and committed men and women.

He was governor of a dozen schools and colleges of further education, and chairman of most of them. He was involved in half a dozen trade union bodies as organiser, representative and negotiator.

If his public image was less vivid than some of his colleagues' it was not for lack of personality. Bill Owen made friends easily and kept them throughout his life. He had no discernible prejudices, racial or social, and he believed in women's rights before the cause became fashionable. He was one of the most popular and respected men in the trade union and labour movements. He could also be "difficult", "obstreperous" and even "downright rude" when he needed to be.

He was a shrewd and committed politician who began his career in local government when newspapers were held at arm's length, and municipal correspondents told no more than was considered necessary. In the late 1960s and early 1970s, when attitudes were changing among council leaders who saw advantage in cultivating the columnists, he was slower than many to lose an ingrained distrust of the "Tory press".

Yet he was not afraid of controversy, earning respect for picking off-beat battles and winning them. He persuaded the council on a free vote to bar circuses featuring live animal acts from Sheffield's public parks. He led campaigns to oppose hare coursing and to ban smoking experiments using dogs. The council followed his lead again in opposing fluoridation of water.

And when he was chairman of the parks committee, he removed "Don't walk on the grass" signs from the city's green spaces - a characteristic touch from a founder member of the Ramblers Association who in his youth had defied landowners to establish the right to walk in Sheffield's golden frame countryside.

Two years before becoming Lord Mayor in 1980, he criticised the incumbent Peter Jackson, the mass media and the Church for their attacks on the trade unions. He believed the unions, especially in the Sheffield region, had done their job in negotiating the best pay and conditions they could get for their members. The steel industry employers had failed in theirs by refusing to invest in modernisation.

Yet he was always fair, even to employers. Asked in 1979 whether the image of hardened steel barons was justified he replied: "They were no worse than their counterparts in other parts of the country. The relationship between the employers and the trade unions collectively was far better than in many other areas."

Bill Owen's energy was prodigious. The Sheffield Morning Telegraph headlined him "Action Man Mayor", a remarkable tribute to a man who had suffered ill health in his childhood, who for a short time attended a school for delicate children. He was a tireless worker as a trade unionist, a politician and a local councillor.

His passionate belief in the values of further education grew out of his own self-directed education as a young school-leaver in the 30s. He read voraciously and loved music, and increasingly argued that the labour movement should retain an interest in cultural activity.

A socialist at the age of 12 - he was growing up when the Labour group on Sheffield city council included Ernest Rowlinson and John Henry Bingham - and an early member of the Young Communist League, he was a committed though not uncritical member of the Labour Party for most of his adult life. "There are too many politicians in the Labour Party and not enough Socialists," he once suggested.

He was given the Freedom of the City in 1991, an honour handed out rarely in Sheffield. There were only 57 other Freemen before him in nearly a century and they included Winston Churchill, Lloyd George, Lord Kitchener, Ramsay MacDonald and Harold Wilson. Bill Owen might not have enjoyed such illustrious company but he would not have been over-awed by them, and few could have doubted his right to the honour.

He was a typical, if outstanding, example of a generation of socialists who grew up in the 1920s and 30s, who educated themselves with the help of the Workers Educational Association and the public libraries, and who talked about the importance of public service and meant it. Most of Bill Owen's service was little seen by the average Sheffielder as he chaired interminable meetings, visited schools, travelled the city from one function to the next.

He was one of the last of the City Fathers, an influential member of the group of elder statesmen and women who had governed Sheffield since 1926 with a break of only one year when Conservative councillors took control in May 1968.

The Labour Group made its mistakes. Hyde Park, The Moor, the Hole in the Road and the city's central roads system have been daily reminders. But Grace Tebbutt, Sidney Dyson, Jim Sterland, Ron Ironmonger, Isidore Lewis, Albert Smith, Patience Sheard, Winifred Golding, Harold Lambert, and their many colleagues gave the people of Sheffield a justifiable pride in a city which enjoyed clean air, green parks, tree-lined streets, and a low-cost, high efficiency transport service.

Bill Owen's last two years were marred by ill health and growing deafness, and there were some, his closest friends among them, who felt he should have stepped down from public life. But he was determined to "die in harness" and he did, on September 25 1992. The evening before he died he attended a meeting of the Labour Group, and in the words of one insider, he was as "outspoken and astute" as he had been through half a century of negotiations, meetings, conferences and rallies.

He left behind friends and admirers who recognised his strengths and accepted his weaknesses - as well as many others who have asked how such a self-effacing, apparently shy man, could have become one of the most influential and effective politicians in Sheffield.

Answering them has not been easy. The best I have been able to do, a year later, is to see Bill Owen through his own eyes and through the memories of his closest friends and colleagues - and to present their words as a collection of portraits, or more accurately, as a series of sketches for a portrait which might eventually be completed.

July 1993

First Thoughts

"I was a political animal from the age of 12. We organised an anti-fascist demonstration against Oswald Moseley when he came to Sheffield and there were 100,000 demonstrators in Barker's Pool and you couldn't move. I sold a thousand copies of the Socialist New Leader that day. When I joined the Communist Party in 1937 I became an outstanding salesman of pamphlets and booklets."

Bill Owen seldom boasted about his achievements as a trade union leader or as a Sheffield city councillor, but he was proud of his record as a street-seller of political pamphlets. He recalled his sales figures clearly in later years, retelling the story to various interviewers as if to re-assert his left-wing credentials.

For those who knew him well in his 35 years as a trade union leader and 40 years as a Labour councillor, no re-assertion was needed. Bill Owen's pedigree was as impeccable as any of his contemporaries. He had grown up in near poverty through the 1920s and 30s, stood in public meetings listening to the leading socialists and communists of the era. He was an activist before his teens, an early member of the Independent Labour Party, the Left Book Club and the Young Communists League. He supported the anti-war movement, the fight against Spanish fascism, the hunger marches and prison reform.

A few months before his death he recalled in an interview : "We were always a political family. We used to have our own debates. My father, even though he voted Labour, was really Conservative and at election time he worked in Hallam for Conservative candidates and got paid for it. He was a friend of the agent because they were in the Buffs together. My mother was a socialist, my eldest brother was in the Communist Party and my second eldest brother in the Co-operative Party."

Bill's father, John Pardoe Owen, was a Black Country man, born in Dudley in 1876. His mother Alice Cole, a domestic worker, was born the same year in London within the sound of Bow bells. John Pardoe worked as a steel leg vicemaker for Allday and Onions in West Bromwich, met and married Alice in 1899, and moved to Sheffield in 1913 to work at Easterbrook Allcard, now Presto Tools.

The Owens already had six children when William and his twin brother George were born on July 7 1914.

"My father was a senior partner in Hoyland Thomas & Company, Mousehole Forge, Malin Bridge. Then he merged with anvil makers in the Rivelin valley, Gregory Bros. He moved into there and formed another company. It was Owen, Thomas & Co - Thomas was a sleeping partner, he was never sober and hardly did any work.

"It was in the 1930s when the recession was bad that the firm went bust. Gregory Brothers were makers of anvils and between them they did very good business for a time but in the end they went bankrupt. My father finished up working for a small tool firm at Heeley Bottom - Hardy Patent Pick.

"When the war broke out he joined up, but they fetched him back because of his occupation. He'd already been measured for his uniform. He was a marvellous bass singer and used to sing with the famous bass Norman Allin in Birmingham. In Sheffield, he was solo bass in the cathedral choir and had his own quartet. He worked until he was 69 when he died of cancer of the bowel."

Bill's eldest brother Charles Philip, his eldest sister Loey, Edward, Bertha and the Owens' first set of twins John Pardoe and Robert Cole were born in the Black Country. With the family settled at 178 Burnaby Street, Walkley, younger sisters Thora and Hilda followed.

When they were five years old, Bill and twin brother George were admitted to Sheffield Children's Hospital where George died of scarlet fever — "We were identical so we don't know to this day whether it was George or Bill who died," Bill told Lillian Munn in a 1985 interview. Bill himself suffered from rickets as a youngster and for a time was a pupil at a special school for delicate children.

"I was actually born in Beeley Wood Road, South Wortley, which was outside the city boundaries then. We moved from there to Walkley. The house is now demolished. It was a terrace type house and there were flags on the floor. We were obviously overcrowded but we were happy - though we certainly weren't rich.

"There was a lot of poverty around at that time. In those days if your class got 100 per cent attendance in the month you got half day on the Friday. Always remember on one occasion the only pair of shoes I'd got had gone to the chap down the road who was a cobbler and he was worse for drink that night so he never mended them. I couldn't go to school the next day, but I remember kids coming and fetching me and carrying me on their backs to school so we got full attendance. I sat in the desk, then they brought me home. By the time I got home my shoes were ready to put on.

"The people around were all working families but on very poor wages. You'd have about £2 a week for a household budget. One neighbour, a Mr Sproson, had a top job as a typographical designer at J G Graves and he also played the flute in an orchestra. His wife unfortunately suffered from a passion for betting on the horses. The woman next door took parcels to the pawnshop, so Sproson's wife took his evening suit that he used for his orchestral work to the pawnshop.

"That Thursday night the shop went up in flames and his suit with it. Sproson was very placid. She'd pawned his suit to back a horse, the horse lost, the suit went up in the fire and he just laughed it off. He was a socialist. So were quite a lot of them at Graves."

The Owens could not afford family holidays, although Bill thought he might have been to the seaside for a day when he was very young, but as he grew into his teens he paid £5 to £10 a week to stay at Lynmouth, Lynton, Penzance and Aberystwyth with a young holiday fellowship, where part of the "payment" was to take turns washing and drying dishes.

"One holiday in Lynmouth I volunteered to do it every day. The manageress was very pleased - she never had such clean pots - could I stay for the season? I said I'm sorry I can't. I've got a job to go to."

As a member of the ILP Guild of Youth he became a rambler, camping in bell tents in the Cordwell Valley. But most of his holidays were spent helping his father work an allotment and sympathising with a neighbour who spent hours building a hut and greenhouse in concrete just before a developer took over the gardens.

He remembered his schooldays with mixed feelings, describing himself in later years as "an 11-plus failure", good at history, scripture, geography and arithmetic, but weak in reading and poetry. Yet he was a prolific reader, the first customer at the first junior library when it opened at Walkley, and a daily visitor there for many years.

"The teacher used to ask us to write down every book we'd read, and they didn't believe me because I'd read that many. They tried to catch me out by asking me to write essays on various books - they were surprised that I could do it.

"I was also good at scripture and on one occasion in junior school a school inspector came to visit. The headteacher then was Miss Styring, a real varmint, but I got on all right with her. Miss Styring called on this pupil and that pupil and they all failed to answer. Her face went red. The inspector said 'Isn't there anyone in this class able to answer the questions?' I put up my hand and said 'Yes sir, I can.' And I did. The teacher was very relieved.

"My strong points were arithmetic and what they called accuracy and intelligence, plus grammar and spelling. It was only later, after I left school, that I started to develop mentally, through the Hillsborough Cooperative Fellowship, Arnold Freeman's Sheffield Educational Settlement, the Workers Educational Association and the National Council of Labour Colleges.

"My mother was the biggest influence on me. She was very good looking, a big woman and very outspoken. Her father was an Irishman working on London docks and he was Keir Hardy's election agent at West Ham when he won the seat. Her father carried her on the shoulder at the dock strike in 1896 led by Tom Burns and Tom Mann - what they called the Docker's Tanner.

"She became very active in the labour and women's movement, became poll captain for the area we lived in. I used to do all the delivering of the Sheffield Co-operator paper. I used to go to Tory election meetings as a school kid and enjoyed hearing the hecklers, not heckling myself, just listening."

He left school in 1928 when he was 14 and for 18 months joined the long ranks of unemployed before he found his first job working in John Holt's pet shop and corn store on South Road, earning 7/6d for a 60 hour week. He proved such an asset that a butcher next door tried to poach him.

"I said I'm going to no abattoir to see animals killed. I didn't like to see animals killed, so I couldn't be a butcher. The corn stores came down for redevelopment. The owner's son Tom opened a store at bottom of Leppings Lane, but it didn't pay and it had to close down. I was out of work and didn't qualify for unemployment benefit because I hadn't enough stamps.

"I got a job as a porter on the railway, but I knew it was only temporary because my eyes weren't good enough. In those days you had to be 100 per cent. Anyway, it was at the time of King George V's Jubilee and they were asking for slogans to improve productivity in the railway industry. I sent one in - 'A1 men for 3C wages'. After that they sent me for a medical and I failed on my eyes. So that finished me.

"It was on the railways I became trade union conscious. Railwaymen in those days were the best trade unionists I've ever known. They were loyal to a man. Only one man in the whole of the Wicker Goods who wasn't in the union and they sent him to Coventry. He had to join in the end, they made his life a misery."

Rejected as unfit for the armed forces when the Second World War began, Bill became manager of the first Workers' Bookshop in Matilda Street, Sheffield. He was already an agent for the Left Book Club with 1000 members on his books and was paid 2/6d a month and 10d back on every book sold.

"My ambition early on was to own my own bookshop. I used to be well in with a bookseller on Devonshire Street called Dickinson. I used to buy lots of second-hand books - and what I didn't want he bought off me. Our regional secretary, Albert Hale, had a marvellous library and was selling them to a London firm but they let him down. I went to his house in Leeds to see them. He wanted £50 and I offered him £45. I got them for the Workers' Bookshop."

The Workers' Bookshop had been financed by an Australian, John Murray, an unsuccessful Labour candidate for Crookesmoor. Murray later returned to Australia, the bookshop was destroyed by a fire, and a second shop was opened on the corner of Rockingham Street by Charlie Easton.

"I worked on a milk round for Sheffield and Ecclesall Co-op in the 1940s until Charlie was called up to work in the Fire Service. He asked me to take the bookshop over so I became manager. When Charlie was released from the Fire Service I still remained manager even though he'd put money into it and it was really his shop."

The bookshop gave Bill long quiet hours for reading William Morris, Ruskin, Walt Whitman, Jack London, Goethe, Upton Sinclair and the poems of William Mather - as well as the opportunity to add to the remarkable collection of trade union and political history books that he would eventually present to the Northern College.

By the time he became an organiser for the Transport and General Workers Union in 1945 he was one of the most widely read and best informed trade unionists in the region.

CHAPTER TWO
In The Blood

If trade unionism was not already in Bill Owen's blood, he was quickly infected by its aims. He joined the Transport and General Workers Union in 1931 when he was 17, surrendered his card when he became a member of the National Union of Railwaymen, and then rejoined in 1935. For the short time he worked as a Sheffield & Ecclesall Co-operative milk roundsman he held dual membership in the T & G and the Union of Shop Distributive and Allied Workers.

He applied for his first full time job with the T & G in 1938 as district secretary for Coventry when the successful applicant was the union's future general secretary, Jack Jones. Bill remembers Ernest Bevin, the general secretary at the time, asking all the candidates to stay behind after the interviews.

"He told us we'd all done well and that the union was looking for members interested in becoming MPs. If we passed the examination he could guarantee us a safe seat. Soon after that I was approached by the leader of the Labour Party in Shipley to be nominated for the constituency. I'd just got the full-time post of organiser in Sheffield so I declined and the man who got the seat became prominent in the Labour government - Creech Jones, Minister for the Colonies. Shipley was a good Labour seat in those days before boundary changes.

"I had ambitions to be in Parliament in the early days but I didn't press it in the end. I got involved in trade unionism."

Bill was still working on his milk round when a vacancy came up for engineering and general trades officer in Sheffield. A friend, Horace Windle, who had fought in the International Brigade, was also applying for a job in the union and Bill "went along to the interview to encourage him." He did little preparation, answering questions from his memory of the union, its rule books and its duties to members.

The interview panel was headed by Arthur Deakin, who had taken over as acting general secretary of the TGWU when Ernest Bevin temporarily relinquished the post to serve as Minister of Labour in the wartime coalition government under Winston Churchill. Bill Owen was offered a job just a month before the war in Europe ended - and Deakin told him later he was "one of the best candidates they ever interviewed".

He became engineering and general trades organiser for a large area covering Sheffield, Mexborough, Conisbrough, Rotherham, Worksop, Chesterfield, Bolsover, and Stocksbridge. When the union reorganised its regional coverage he became Sheffield's first district secretary, heading the biggest trade union in the area, with over 30,000 members on his books.

Bill Owen photographed in Sanpene, Italy on his birthday in 1947 - two years after he became District Officer of the TGWU.

The honeymoon with Deakin did not last. Bill's independent mind and forthright left wing opinions were not compatible with Deakin's policies, described by the young organiser as "a cautious approach to wages and a ruthless approach to any progressive thought in the union".

"I was at variance with union policy right up to the time when Frank Cousins took over the leadership in 1955, but I was fortified by the fact that there were such officers as Cousins around who were of my way of thinking and who gave me great moral support. On occasions I had to change my line of action but there was no compulsion to change my line of thinking, and I never did."

Through the late 1920s and 30s, his political beliefs had been maturing. He joined the ILP Guild of Youth in 1931 - "It was one of the finest youth bodies that was ever founded" - and campaigned vigorously during the years the ILP was affiliated to the Labour Party.

To Bill Owen, the ILP was a "brotherhood of man - idealistic", formed in 1893, a full 20 years before the Labour Party. In the 1922 General Election the ILP group of MPs increased from five to 22. There were differences in approach between the two affiliated parties, but no animosity until the ILP voted to disaffiliate in 1936 - "the biggest mistake we ever made" in Bill's opinion.

The Guild of Youth had been formed at York in 1924, and by December 1925 had 171 branches. Catering for young people aged 14 to 21, the Guild organised football leagues, swimming, hiking and discussion groups. With its decline, large numbers moved en bloc to the Communist Party.

Bill Owen chaired open-air meetings for the ILP, one of them attracting 1000 people outside Weston Park. It was in full-throated swing when an appeal came from Winter Street sanatorium - the patients were finding it impossible to sleep.

His friends included Wilfred Wigham, one of three famous sons of Quaker missionaries. Born in China, Wigham was political editor of the Sheffield Independent before joining Arnold Freeman's Sheffield Educational Settlement as printer. He later became General Secretary of the ILP.

"My idols were Jimmy Maxton, George Buchanan, Campbell Stevens and John Wheatley, who became Minister of Health in the 1924 Labour government. Buchanan was the expert on benefits - he could recite all the benefits people were entitled to. They were my heroes - known as the Clydeside Four.

"I remember campaigning for Florence Williams who was a Labour councillor for Manor. She stood on the ILP ticket and Jimmy Maxton came down in a small car. I took him on Wybourn and the big crowds were aghast at his oratory, he was that brilliant. He was in the teaching profession, Campbell Stevens was a parson, George Buchanan a moulder.

"George Fletcher, the Sheffield master baker, was standing for the Communist Party in the Manor against Florence Williams. In those days you would chalk on pavements announcing meetings and on one occasion we'd chalked a meeting at the same time the Communist Party had chalked down a meeting for George Fletcher. They were both pinched and fined in the courts.

"I went up to Clydeside for a parliamentary election and was taken to a central committee room. They said when you go knocking on the doors be very careful. You'll be asked 'Are you a Billy or a Danny?' Say you're a Danny or they'll lynch you.' Billy meant you were a Protestant, Danny was the Catholic vote."

After the break between the ILP and Labour Party, Bill joined the Communist Party, resigning in 1949 to join the Labour Party.

"I became an outstanding salesman of pamphlets and booklets and at the time of Italy's invasion of Abyssinia I organised a party of six to sell pamphlets at the top of Dixon Lane and other points around. In two hours we sold over 1000 copies at 1d a copy."

Soon after the Left Book Club was started by Victor Gollancz in 1939, Bill became the club's representative in Sheffield and again showed remarkable selling skills. When John Strachey published his 2d pamphlet "Why I Am A Socialist", Bill sold 10,000 copies throughout South Yorkshire.

His first few years as T & G district secretary taught Bill Owen that the job was primarily to prevent disputes starting rather than trying to solve them later. "I learned to be a peacemaker rather than agitator," he said. His first test as a full-time officer plunged him straight into three simultaneous strikes, however.

"One of the biggest problems was at Steetley Company where the kiln burners had been out 48 hours and wanted to stay out to have Christmas at home. But kilns work seven days a week and the dolomite would have been ruined if we didn't get the workers back. It finished up with my regional secretary Albert Hale going round using a loudspeaker calling them to a meeting. He was outstanding. He got them back to work straight away, otherwise there was £50,000 worth of dolomite going to waste.

"I remember a strike of busmen in Sheffield and I hired the City Hall for a meeting. To get in you had to show your trade union card. Albert Hale addressed the meeting and a busman pushed up to the platform to put his teeth in Albert's wrist. Albert was a big strong man, had been a boxer in his younger days, and he lifted his arm and swung him off. The busman landed on the floor. Albert went on speaking and he got them back to work. He had all the full-time officers with him on the platform but he did all the spouting. He knew all the tricks. To hear him speak you would think he was 200 years old because of the different jobs he had had.

"While we were different politically - he was more on the right and I was more on the left - he stood by you, even if you made a mistake. He would rollock you privately but would stick by you. He would not admit your mistake publicly. He was loyal, and it was a lesson I learned."

Well established as T & G district secretary by 1960, Bill was able to indulge himself with little fear of "rollocking" from above. He combined his love of music and his lifelong support for the persecuted when he invited the outstanding black American singer Paul Robeson and his wife to join Mr and Mrs Frank Cousins as guests of honour at the union's annual dinner and dance on March 30.

"Robeson used to sing at the Left Book Club rallies in London at the Royal Albert Hall and I met him by attending the rallies. I invited him to our union dinner and to my surprise he came. Over 1000 sat down to dinner in Sheffield City Hall and we could have sold the tickets three times over. Robeson was persuaded to respond to the toast and you could hear a pin drop. He recited from Othello and sang - marvellous, what a voice. Everybody went into raptures. He fetched the place down.

"There had been some problems in America because of his Communist links and he said he accepted our invitation because of the influence our union had brought to get his release from America. He booked himself in at the Grand Hotel and he had a suite. When I asked him if we could cover the cost he said 'Bill are you trying to insult me?

" 'I don't want a penny and shall be offended if you attempt to persuade me. Your union came to me when I was in need of friends. This is one of the ways I can repay you.' He paid all his own expenses."

CHAPTER THREE

Owen's Law

Working with Bill Owen in the Transport and General Workers Union offices in Hartshead, in countless committees, and in frequent face to face negotiations with employers, was an education and a challenge for his colleagues. It could sometimes be a frustrating experience as well, calling for patience, an agile, alert mind, and a feel for logistics.

Albert Bedford's close relationship with Bill began in 1967 with "marriage" talks between the Sheffield Amalgamated Union of File Trades and the T & G. When they were completed in 1970, the file trade general secretary became the enlarged union's district organiser for the engineering and allied trades. He succeeded Bill as district secretary in 1979, retiring in 1990.

Born in Sheffield in 1927, in a house on the Moor where the Training Enterprise and Education Directorate building now stands, Albert Bedford came from a family of miners - his father and seven uncles all worked at local pits. He attended Park Council School in Duke Street, started work at Turton Brothers & Matthews in the metallurgical office, but soon started an apprenticeship as a file cutter with Henry Stones & Sons. After serving in the Royal Navy as a stoker he returned to his old job for 27 years. When he became general secretary of the File Trades union in 1967, there were still 32 companies in his area. By amalgamation, only 16 companies remained in a rapidly declining industry, and officials concluded they could offer members a better service as an autonomous section of the T & G.

Albert Bedford

" I soon realised that Bill was unique in negotiations. A lot of people thought he wasn't listening because he had a habit of holding his head and partly closing his eyes, but he never missed a thing. He was a very astute individual. He was a good negotiator but from time to time he used to upset employers by his attitude, because people thought he was a bit offhand. In fact, a lot of the members thought he was offhanded, but he wasn't. He was

100 per cent in everything he said, because he was a trade unionist through and through. But he had a very dry humour. When his first wife Joan was out, he used to take their white poodle with him to meetings. I've never known anybody else go to industrial negotiations and take their pet poodle so obviously - but nobody objected.

When he was in negotiations he made copious notes. He could pick points and he knew when to say something and when not to say something. He could put forward a balanced case and I think that was the main reason for his success. He knew how to balance a case without going over the top. He knew what his bottom line was and he was realistic.

He was a listener, but if he felt someone was pulling wool over his eyes he could be very vitriolic. In fact, in his bluntness he could be rude and I've seen him upset employers. But he wasn't a physical person, he hadn't got a physical presence. Over the years he had a rapport with employers, particularly with the engineering employers, because he was also the district secretary of the Confederation of Shipbuilding and Engineering Unions.

I worked with him for 25 years and went to a lot of meetings with him in that time. I remember going to KP Nuts in Rotherham for a meeting in the canteen - all ladies actually - and we were reporting back on the wage negotiations. Sometimes, as union officers, you have to tell people things they don't like and on this occasion we had to tell the membership that we couldn't achieve what they thought they were entitled to. Bill was standing on a table in the canteen and there was a surge of women and he finished up on his back. We had to catch him falling off the table. There were problems like this from time to time, but he never shirked his responsibilities. In some instances he was fairly blunt. But when you got to know him he was a gentleman.

Of course his job gave him power. But I used to say it wasn't Bill Owen or Albert Bedford going into a place, it was a Transport and General Workers Union officer. When Bill was district secretary there was tremendous power, because if he wanted to he could cause problems. But he used to exercise that power in a realistic and honest way. We all knew if we abused it we could create problems for our members.

Bill had a lot of influence as well - we used to talk about 'Owen's Law'. If any problems came up when he was in the chair and someone challenged his ruling, Bill could always say 'Well, in nineteen so and so, rule so and so was amended' so that it would fit in with his point of view. Bill had been at it that long, nobody else knew, nobody could challenge him. So everybody used to say 'That's Owen's Law'. Some of the rulings were genuine but it got to such a stage that people wanted all the standing orders and rules and regulations laid down. There were quite a few battles with the district committee of the TGWU when he used to state the reasons why he couldn't accept resolutions.

He never drove a car - he took lessons but he didn't pass - but he had worked out a system, and when I say he was unique I mean he got away with murder.

I used to drive him to different places - not only me but all the other officers, and not only officers of the TGWU but people like George Caborn who was the AUEW district secretary and Ernest Johnson, EETPU. He used to have employers come and pick him up. If they rang him up and asked him to a meeting, he'd say 'I'll come if you'll pick me up', which was a bit unusual to say the least. He used to turn out at Chapel en le Frith to the Ferodo factory before I took the place over, and he used to travel on the train to Chinley and the company met him with a chauffeur-driven car.

But it never put him under any obligation. Definitely not. Bill was under no obligation to anybody. In fact, he used to take it as a right, and he used to organise his diary around the other officers' diaries. Before he set up any meetings of his own he used to look at all the diaries and if they coincided with places he wanted to go to he would fix his meeting and then arrange to be dropped off.

He was a very political animal, even more than he was industrial. But his

council work didn't interfere with his job. At the time he first came into the
T&G a lot of the negotiations were done at national level so it was just a
question of interpreting what the national agreement said. But from 1969,
when the district committees were set up, when Jack Jones became general
secretary, the negotiations were done mainly at plant level. That meant the
officers used to deal with the negotiations first and if they got into any
difficulties referred it up to national level. But Bill used to do a lot of his work
through correspondence rather than meeting people across the table. He spent
9-5 in the office so if he did council work he was invariably in the office at
night. He never neglected his work, but obviously from time to time his
colleagues had to assist him. We worked as a team and we knew what he was
doing, particularly Bill and I, because we covered similar industries.

I'd be stretching truth if I said the other officers were always happy about
it. Obviously they did it, but if it conflicted with something they wanted to do
they used to tell him. In any office or factory sometimes things get on top of
you and people let off steam, but overall it was fine. If anyone said 'No,
because I've got X Y Z' he accepted it. From time to time he used to tell them
what to do but overall he was good at team work.

We had engineering disputes when they had shorter working weeks, we had
the road transport dispute in 1974 and obviously we were involved in the 1974
miners' dispute because we had membership in the mining industry. We also
got involved in the Common Market referendum which was orchestrated
mainly through the union because the TGWU was anti-Common Market.

For four or five years after the referendum we were still anti-Market but we
realised there was no way we were going to come out, so we then started to
work to improve the benefits we would get from the Common Market. Bill
could be flexible, even in politics. We all came from rough backgrounds and
we all wanted to alter the system. The Communist Party was very insular
because everything was against them at that time so they had to be insular.

As Bill got a bit older, just as we all did, he wanted to alter everything and he knew he couldn't do that outside the system. He had to get inside and the logical place to do it was through the Labour Party. But his basic principles never altered. He wanted to redress the balance between what was happening to the poor side of society and what was happening to the more affluent side of the community.

Bill and I had a good working relationship. We were a duo, wherever one went the other was there. Outside the office we were friends, and my wife Florence got on very well with his first wife, Joan. She was very supportive of what Bill did, much to her detriment really. She put him first and foremost. Whatever his activities she would fall in line and if she thought somebody wasn't treating him in the way he should be treated because of his position she was very soon able to complain. She was a very loyal person.

When she was ill we took them to Scarborough a couple of times, because they never had a car and Bill wanted to get her out of the house. He was lonely after Joan died and for a while he was quite lost. Mind you he had good colleagues, and his ward party in Walkley, particularly Dorothy and Barry Whittington, were very good and loyal to him.

I learned patience from Bill, particularly in negotiations. I learned to do my homework before going into any negotiation, and to have things written down so I wasn't struggling to remember - inflation figures, profits of the company and all the elements which enable you to put forward a reasonable case. He was meticulous in that respect. When you work with people like Bill you learn, either wittingly or unwittingly.

I think his biggest contribution in Sheffield was the introduction of democracy at local level by encouraging the shop stewards to work to their own abilities, to resolve problems within their own workshops and offices. He thought that by advancing their abilities it would enhance the reputation of the union. And you would also satisfy the membership because their problems would be dealt with on a day to day basis rather than waiting until an officer was available.

Education was important in the union. We had a college at Cirencester at that time, covering economics, politics, history, negotiation and representation. Locally there were shop stewards courses. And there was a lot of legislation from the 60s onwards - health and safety, the Equal Pay Act, industrial relations - so we set up seminars and workshops to take people through all aspects of the changes, a tremendous amount of work. It was all part of the job. When you were a full-time officer you had to give spiritual advice, you had to be a solicitor, you had to be a good all-rounder in fact.

When Bill retired he became Lord Mayor and that was ideal for him because there was no sudden breaking off and worrying what he'd do when he retired. He had a special evening for the trade unions and invited representatives from all the unions. He also invited his namesake Bill Owen, the actor who played Compo in Last of the Summer Wine, because he was an honorary member of the fire brigade union. And there was another Bill Owen who was an alderman in Rotherham and also a retired T & G officer. It was a funny evening. Everyone was talking about Bill Owen but they didn't know which Bill Owen they meant there were so many of them knocking about that night. **""**

Heide Wiedemann was Bill Owen's secretary, stayed on in the same job with his successor Albert Bedford, and is still with the T & G's present district secretary, Keith Garner. Born in Germany, she spent some years in Ireland, before moving to Sheffield to work for the union.

"" He always said I forced his hand and made him employ me because I had been offered a job at Lodge Moor at the same time, and I made him make up his mind straight away. I stayed on, and I'm still here after 26 years. I found it a little difficult at the beginning because I'd never worked for anybody like Bill Owen. I hadn't worked for a trade union or anything, and he lived his life for the trade union and the Labour Party.

It took me a few years to get to know what he was really like. He was very even tempered, but he could lose his temper. We had the odd row - mostly on

Bill's official press photograph as Lord Mayor of Sheffield

Heide Wiedemann

my side because in some ways he could be unreasonable. I can't even remember what the rows were about but there was never any animosity after them.

He could be grumpy if things didn't suit him and he could be awkward - we've blessed him more often than not. But on the whole he was quite an easy person to work for. We understood each other. He always said as long as I did the work he wanted it didn't matter what way I did it. Most of it was union work, but there was the occasional bit for the Labour Group or for the trades council.

When his first wife Joan died he was really cut up, but he coped very well. He wasn't one that really showed his feelings. I think he felt a lot more than he ever showed. He had a sort of facade so that you never knew exactly what he was thinking and it used to amuse me at meetings. I used to attend the district committees of the union with him and he'd be sitting at the top table practically horizontal. But nothing escaped him. He had heard absolutely everything.

Last year we contacted him about something that had happened years ago and he knew the details exactly. He had a fantastic memory. He always kept in touch. He used to walk in, sit down and we ran circles round him - he never changed. He didn't even look any different.

He worked tremendously hard and never seemed to go home. Joan Owen used to say she only saw him in the late evenings and perhaps for breakfast. He used to tell us he had a pint of porridge in the mornings made with a pint of milk and that's what kept him going, but I honestly don't know how he kept it up.

In those days all the officers were called Mister. It seems to have relaxed lately, and after he retired we used to call him Bill. He used to send us a Christmas card, invariably the Sheffield City Council Christmas card, and he used to come round selling them as well, but he didn't remember our birthdays, although he was always pleased when we remembered his. We made him buy cream buns as the rest of us did on our birthdays - he didn't get away with it. **" "**

Sylvia Greenwood became an officer of the TGWU in 1980, a year after Bill Owen retired. She initially covered the engineering section but later changed her remit to the food and drink and women's sections.

She met Bill in 1968 when she was a GMB shop steward at GEC in Mexborough. In 1972 she moved to Sheffield after her marriage broke down and Bill immediately contacted her to offer support. A year later she joined the T & G and started work at Easterbrook and Allcard on Penistone Road - a non-union factory for 20 years.

" I started organising there in March 1973, picking up 600 members, and in the October I was dismissed for trade union activity. Bill was my officer at that time and during the four weeks we were on strike he allowed us to use his office, negotiated for us and we won the dispute. I went back into the factory and became the convenor of an all-male shop stewards committee. Becoming a full-time officer was as a result of my experience there - Bill always said I was his protege because he guided me through all those years.

Sylvia Greenwood

There was a lot of pressure during the strike. I remember the company made a statement that I was 'a communist infiltrator sent by George Caborn to ferment unrest', which was rather funny because we were T & G, not AEU, and the statements in the press about the company scraping bottom of barrel trying to discredit me all came from Bill. And at the end of the day Bill helped win the battle by his skill in negotiation.

For weeks the media delve into your personal background, about your breakdown of marriage and where you were living, and private detectives try to dig up personal and political dirt on you. I would often go home and be physically sick, because I knew I was responsible for people losing money - and they were people on low pay to start with. The kind of support that Bill

Owen gave me will stay with me the rest of my life. It's not just that he was doing his job as an officer. He gave psychological support by talking it through, standing with you, believing in you, and helping you to overcome all obstacles.

Bill was very good at utilising people as well, getting them to help out with other problems around the area. If he had a welfare problem he'd rope you in to deal with it, whether it was Chileans or some woman who'd left her husband and was in distress. He'd ring you up and say 'I want you to come along and assist,' and before you knew what you were at, you were doing it. That was his way of dealing with things.

He rang me up again when we had some members in dispute at Grosvenor House Hotel. We'd organised them and the company had got rid of them. Bill reminded me that these were women who needed support and there were very few active women in the organisation back in the 70s. He suggested I go down and show support on the picket line. I had the 'flu, but one could never turn him down, so about five or six o'clock on a Sunday night I got in my car and went down. Jim Holmes who was an officer at that time had agreed with the police a picket line of six or seven people, but there was a mass picket taking place.

As I started to walk to picket line, the doors of a van opened suddenly and out swooped the police. I hadn't actually got to the picket line when all the police started running. They were behaving quite arrogantly and pushing people, and I was saying 'Move. As long as you move you're not breaking the law of obstruction.' One policeman was pushing me in the back and I said 'Don't push me, the law doesn't say that you have a right to push me, it says I have a right to move.' He said 'If you open your mouth again I'm going to have you,' so I said 'If you want to take me, take me,' so he did. They got hold of Bill Owen and he contacted a solicitor because I was arrested down at police station.

After that, Bill suggested I plead guilty to obstruction, although I objected strongly because I was only moving to my car. But he said 'Look, if you don't plead guilty you'll never become a magistrate.' I told him in no way did I intend to become a magistrate, and on principle I wasn't prepared to plead guilty. He accepted my argument and arranged representation for me and we ended up in court where I was told I was technically guilty of obstruction, although the magistrate accepted I was trying to get to my car. There was no fine but the union could afford to pay the costs and so they should. That's an example of Bill Owen getting you involved in things and you ending up with problems!

That was his typical way. If there was a problem, he'd involve anybody and everybody, and he had a way of making us feel that we had an obligation to him. Obviously we responded. This wasn't just an office like it is now, because Bill used it to organise things. The Chileans would meet here, we had welfare benefits here, we had People's March For Jobs - they used our office and telephones and Bill was always there to help anybody.

He was an absolutely amazing man. When his first wife Joan was ill he'd sometimes give me the job of ringing her up to check that she was okay, but mostly so that she could have somebody to talk to. And I remember he gave me a bed when I got my first council house after I'd been in furnished accommodation - this is the type of welfare that Bill would think about. They were the things that are over and above being an officer, they were about what the man was. If there was a bent reed anywhere, or a broken reed, somebody who had real emotional or financial problems, you can bet Bill would be there finding somebody to assist, and they didn't have to be a T & G member.

A lot of my trade union welfare work that makes me a bit different is a result of Bill broadening my horizons. He was aware that I could be used, he'd sussed that out. He knew what he could draw from you and what he couldn't draw from you. Any success I have is as a result of his guidance. He was responsible for me becoming a member of an industrial tribunal, and I've been on tribunals since 1975 as a lay person. And he would put me forward not just because I was a woman, but because I had ability which was proven. That was before women were selected because they were women. I've never ever been the token woman. I was elected to district committee and then onto national committee of T & G Engineering Section. I became one of the first full-time woman officers. There were no positive places for women, there never have been in our union.

Outside work I could never fathom him. You never knew what Bill was thinking. I didn't see much of him socially except for the trades council dinner and dance. He lived and breathed his trade union and his politics and so the only time that you'd see Bill outside of office would be at those kind of places, and all the time he'd be circulating round, talking to people, and then he'd see someone else and move on. It never stopped. He never seemed to unwind from it, you never saw him just himself - well, I don't know what himself was all the years I've known him.

Only once, just before Joan died, I was talking to him and he said 'When I think about it, she's been the most tolerant person, because all I've ever done is what I do,' and that was the time when he was really sad. I went to Joan's funeral and I think it was the first time I saw him in a grief-stricken situation. I didn't think he'd notice me, but he knew everybody who'd been there. I sat at the back but he had noticed I was there. **,, ,,**

Portraits of a City Father

CHAPTER FOUR

The Caborn-Owen Axis

As trade unionists, Bill Owen and George Caborn were virtually inseparable. There were few trades council or joint union meetings where one would be seen without the other, usually arriving together, with George chauffeuring. If Bill Owen was president or chairman, George was often secretary. When they reversed roles on No 28 District Committee of the Confederation of Shipbuilding and Engineering Unions, with George as chairman and Bill as secretary, there was no detectable weakening in their unanimity of purpose.

They were both senior figures on the influential Sheffield Trades Council, Bill as president and George as secretary of its economic and employment subcommittee. Both were governors of Sheffield Polytechnic, Bill as chairman or deputy chairman, George as chairman of the personnel committee. And both were honoured by the Poly with honorary fellowships. George was also president of Sheffield Campaign Against Racism and chairman of the local Manpower Services Commission special programmes committee.

"Sheffield is a unique city," George Caborn believed. "Everybody knows one another and you can't kid them. If you take three or four hundred people in this city, covering all aspects - management, trade unions, education, you name it - these people come together again and again. You don't realise the sort of team there is holding Sheffield together."

Like his close ally on that team, George Caborn was a complex personality. But like Bill Owen, too, he was widely trusted and respected as a maker of agreements that both employers and employees knew would not be broken - not by him. The district secretary of the mighty Amalgamated Union of Engineering Workers for over 12 years was variously described as a tough, straight-talking trade unionist, a lifelong Communist who could be angry and aggressive with those he thought fools, warm and friendly with those he respected. He was in turn "a militant trade unionist from the grass roots of the movement" and "an elder statesman" of it.

Born in Attercliffe on July 14 1916, he grew up in the same era of high unemployment, low wages and social deprivation as Bill Owen. His father, like Bill's, was in employment when others were not, a second generation craftsman whose job as foreman manager at Sanderson Brothers ensured the family were relatively better off than many of their neighbours. Yet, when he left Woodbourn Road School at 14, George was told there would be no job for him at Sandersons.

"You have got to get a job on your own merit, my father told me, and I did," George told journalists who interviewed him shortly before his retirement. Then he added that it was his talent as a footballer and cricketer that tipped the balance in his favour when he applied for an apprenticeship at Firth Brown, a company which valued sporting success highly. "There were a lot of youngsters out of work. I was lucky, I was bloody lucky. I have been lucky all my life."

George Caborn - "He overshadowed everyone else."

By the age of 22 he was a shop steward, and a year later a convenor, enthusiastic but inexperienced, making his share of mistakes as he honed his negotiating skills head to head with Sir John Green, director of Firth Brown's personnel department and chairman of the Engineering Employers' Federation.

"He was a hard nut to crack, and you found out very quickly that you have to know your business with a bloke like that. He was scrupulously honest and if he said something you could depend on it. I remember getting him to agree to a revision of prices. He did not realise the work he was creating to get it all done. The next time he saw me he said 'One up to you. Didn't I drop a clanger?' But he never tried to go back on his word."

The young trade unionist was determined to live up to that standard. "No matter what ideological approach you might have, if you're going to be a trade union negotiator and you are going to strike bargains, sometimes good, sometimes bad, both parties have got to have standards of conduct. The bargain has to be kept," he insisted.

George Caborn certainly kept his ideological bargain with the Communist Party, serving on its executive for eight years, refusing to apologise for his beliefs when the party was widely criticised during the Hungarian uprising and other crises. "I joined the Communist Party in 1941 and experienced the golden years after the war. The Party made some horrible mistakes of a sectarian character. It makes you shudder now. We thought we were God's chosen children - we had such arrogance."

In 1960, when his shop steward's credentials were removed in a disagreement with his union's hierarchy, he was dropped from the AEUW's district committee. Accepting advice from a veteran socialist colleague not to seek injunctions against his union, he fought his way back within the union structure, defeating the sitting candidate to become the engineering workers' district president and, nine years later, district secretary of the AEU.

He made few enemies and most of them found their bitterness evaporate in face of George Caborn's stubborn integrity. When he was given the Freedom of the City in January 1982, leading Tory councillors boycotted the ceremony. He ignored them and enjoyed what he described as one of the highlights of his life surrounded by friends, his wife Mary and his two sons David, a teacher at Earl Marshal school, and Richard, now MP for Sheffield Central. Five months later, the reaction of shocked friends and adversaries to his sudden death on June 15 was unanimous.

"The Freedom was the pinnacle for him and the one tribute that touched him more than anything else," said Richard Caborn. "One of the nice things about it - and about the letters that my mum received when he died - was the broad spectrum of respect for him. That would also be said about Bill Owen, but Bill died when he was out of the limelight. My dad died just ten months after he retired. From the Chief Constable all the way through - everybody respected him."

To Nick Kemp, the engineering employers' leader, George Caborn was "absolutely straight and honest, a very able negotiator." Dr George Tolley, principal of Sheffield City Polytechnic, described him as "one of the most genuine people I have ever met," and Jack Illingworth, chairman of Firth Brown's shop stewards' committee, said "George was the one that got off his backside and got cracking. My wife and I always said George worked himself to death for the movement - and that was before he died."

George Caborn is still remembered in Sheffield and, when old friends talk of him, the affection and admiration can still be heard in their voices. Shortly before his own death, Bill Owen spoke of his old friend and ally as "probably the most outstanding trade union leader in this city. He overshadowed everyone else."

The city commemorated him in its own way in May 1983, when a small triangle of derelict land at the junction of Spital Hill and Carlisle Street was landscaped and renamed "Caborn's Corner". A plaque was unveiled at the spot from which George had traditionally led demonstrations and rallies.

Among the politicians, trade unionists and friends at the unveiling was his son Richard, MP for Sheffield Central and Chairman of the House of Commons Select Committee for Trade and Industry. Richard left school at 15 and was apprenticed as a fitter at Firth Brown. Emulating his father, he was shop steward at 21, convener at 23, and he was later elected to the executives of the Sheffield Labour Party and the trades council. A Member of the European Parliament before moving to Westminster, his close association with Bill Owen began when they worked together on the 1964 municipal election and the General Election of 1966.

Richard Caborn

❝ I've actually known Bill Owen since I was a little child. He used to run the bookshop for the Communist Party at the top of Matilda Street and I used to go in there on a Saturday morning with my dad. When he became a trade union official I came into contact with him a lot both socially and through the trade union and Labour movement.

What symbolised Bill Owen for me was his deep commitment to education. He saw that the quality of life was enhanced by education, the appreciation of culture, the appreciation of literature. He made a tremendous contribution to Sheffield in those areas. At the same time he was involved in the trade union movements, the protest movements. Whether it was the campaign for nuclear disarmament, anti-apartheid or general liberation and a safer world, he applied his practical socialist principles. He was one of the main collectors for the International Brigade. When Jack Jones and others were fighting in Spain, Bill was collecting money and clothing, and arguing the political case for supporting the International Brigade against Franco when the British government wouldn't do anything.

An official engagement with Fred Mulley MP, the Lord Mayor (Albert Smith), George Brown MP and Mrs Smith, the Lady mayoress

Bill was a great motivator in this city. He was a fixer, and I don't say that in the critical sense. Bill would do his homework, then he did his groundwork, and then he would deliver. Before he went into the Labour group or an education committee or a trades council executive, he would have the votes in the bag. Many, many meetings took place in Bill Owen's office at Transport House with the officers of the trades council and District Labour Party to ensure that the movement marched hand in hand.

Bill spanned trade unions and the Labour Party, and he was unique in the way he could balance those forces and encourage the most progressive policies for the area, as he saw them. That's where his strengths lay, in being able to convince people at a personal and private level so they would effect the decisions.

Quality of housing, quality of the health service - again Bill was in the forefront. He led the Labour Party and the trades council for more than 25 years, and he worked very closely with my dad in those areas and on the Confederation of Shipbuilding and Engineering Workers where George was the president and Bill was the secretary. The Confed covered all the unions in Sheffield, Chesterfield, North East Derbyshire, so they were a formidable force. All the major engineering employers had a great respect for Bill and George because when they went in to do a deal - good, bad or indifferent - they knew that deal would last. There would be no breaking of agreements. They had basic principles, a basic ethos, and they worked very closely together to hold principles and ethos together.

They always said to me 'You're dealing with some of the most skilled engineers and artisans and professions in any major city in this country.' They were very proud of our skill base and they protected it. That's why we had more further education colleges than any other major city, that's why we had the second biggest polytechnic in the country. They saw FE as a means of educating working class people both for a fuller life and also for a trade. They were very keen on apprentice training, and they also saw it was necessary to bring the employers and the trade unions together as we did on many boards of governors in the FE colleges. I think that has held Sheffield in extremely good stead.

Beyond that, they used to bring together the leading convenors, full-time trade union officers, leaders of the Doncaster, Barnsley, Rotherham and Chesterfield councils, to discuss the area's problems and hopefully find solutions. There is no doubt that those two men dominated the movement. Bill was the district secretary of the T&G and George Caborn district secretary for the AEU. When the two unions worked in unison you had a formidable force. They were frequently consulted by national leaders and the Caborn-Owen axis in Sheffield was not dissimilar to the Scanlon-Jones axis at TUC level.

They worked together organising meetings in Sheffield with national figures like Aneurin Bevan and Jennie Lee speaking at them. I remember when I was at Prince Edward School I was called in to see the headmaster after assembly, and I thought Good God what have I done now? I went in and he said 'Could your father get me two tickets for the Bevan meeting?' That's how coveted they were.

George understood Bill's reasons for leaving the Communist Party and that shows another characteristic of both of them. They were pragmatic, never dogmatic, and that led them into some hellish difficulties - there are many stories about their being accused of selling out. But they had basic principles - once you struck a deal that was it, you worked for the highest common factor not the lowest common denominator. They were prepared to sit down with the employers and try to get the best for Sheffield, because it was Sheffield they worked for. To that end they were pragmatic politicians. They were also good friends. They were great lovers of music and they mixed together socially quite a lot. Neither of them drank very much. If Dad had a glass of lager and Bill had a glass of wine that was it. So when we all used to go to the pub after meetings, Bill and George came only occasionally, depending on the occasion.

Bill was never over-earnest, he just led a very simple life. In his later years he did go abroad, but he was never one for the high life. He was a very withdrawn character, unless you got him into a situation where his convictions came out and then he was a different man altogether. He was never one of the city's flamboyant characters and he wasn't an orator, unlike my dad. In some respects they complemented one another, because there weren't many meetings that they were not together.

I got the impression that Bill was an atheist, a bit like my father in the sense that he had his own beliefs but more or less kept them to himself. He would discuss them with you but he wouldn't go out and put them on his cuff. My mother was a very strong Methodist, still is today, and she used to play the organ at the church. I was the first person to take an alcoholic drink into our house at the age of 21. Yet I had a father who was an executive member of the Communist Party. The circle of people our family moved in ranged from Harry Pollitt and Willy Gallagher to Donald Soper. Some would say it was extremely contradictory but it's not. My dad respected my mum's beliefs and my mum respected my dad's, and that made them as compatible as possible.

Religion was not important to Bill and George, was not a part of their lives. But they knew that there were some very strong groupings particularly from the Methodist and the radical wing of the Christian movement in the Labour movement and they worked hard to keep them on board.

Bill was different from most of his contemporaries on the council. He was much more radical. He was a product of the Communist Party, the Marxist philosophy, in his early days. He was far better read than any of those other contemporary leaders. My dad was extremely well read as well, and they were intellectual giants at that time. Things have changed since then, but at that time they were respected for their intellect, their honesty, their credibility. Their radicalism manifested itself in practical propositions like fighting for education, comprehensive education, the cheap bus fares policy, sound housing policy. That was practical socialism, redistribution of wealth in a very practical way. I think the thing that dismayed Bill Owen most about centralisation of government was its anti-democratic nature. Because Bill was a democrat, and he believed in decision-making at the lowest possible level. What he saw was not just resources shrinking but the power for people to enable and activate being taken away.

Bill believed in enablement of ordinary people. Education was part of that process of enabling, and Bill's greatest contribution was in education. Without Bill Owen and his great vision of having an institution like Ruskin College we might not have had the Northern College. He called Michael Barratt Brown, George Caborn, Peter Horton, Royden Harrison and myself together to discuss plans for the college and we did it through the further and adult education subcommittee which Bill chaired. We decided that not only did we want it but we started looking for sites. We had a lot of contact with Shirley Williams and she was enthusiastic about it and helped us immensely.

Education was the great liberator of the working class to Bill and he was totally committed to the development of further education colleges, comprehensive education, the Polytechnic and Northern College. There was very little happened on the education scene without Bill Owen. You had Peter Horton, the academic, as chairman of the education committee balanced by Bill Owen, the working class person who was probably one of the best read, best self-educated people in the city. **"**

Portraits of a City Father

CHAPTER FIVE
Two Streams -
One Mighty River

When Bill Owen succeeded Joe Madin as president of Sheffield Trades Council and the District Labour Party in 1960, he was as well versed in their history and as aware of their influence in the city as any of their 250 or more trade union and political delegates. He had written the first chapter of the book that celebrated the Council's centenary in 1958. Co-authors John Mendelson, a university lecturer and later MP for Penistone, Vernon Thornes, the recently-appointed secretary to the council, and the book's editor Dr Sidney Pollard provided the rest.

The opening lines of "The Forerunners" found Bill Owen in lyrical mood. "The Trades and Labour Council traces its origin to two sources: the trade unions and the political organisations of the labouring classes," he wrote. "In the course of their history these two streams seldom ran parallel: at one time one would swell, apparently absorbing all the waters, while the other disappeared underground ... it is only in recent years that the two streams have combined in one mighty river."

That mighty river had begun life in 1858 as the Sheffield Association of Organised Trades, and it was not until after the First World War that the trades council made its appearance.

The SAOT's first secretary was William Dronfield, a printer and well known radical in his day. Its treasurer was the publican William Broadhead, soon to be involved in the "rattening" scandals which led to the Royal Commission investigation into the systematic intimidation of craftsmen who were defying the authority of trade societies. The "Sheffield Outrages" did little to help the image of trade unionism but the fledgling organisation survived to rebuild its reputation and expand its influence.

By the 1950s, the trades council was involved in employment, training and careers. Its members were governors of colleges and schools, and were represented on national insurance and industrial tribunals. At one stage, secretary Thornes counted over 200 trades council members holding one or more places on various bodies, and Bill Owen held more of them than anyone else. Campaigns were run to create more jobs and training places for the post-war bulge of school leavers - and to safeguard jobs which were disappearing with the rapid introduction of new technology in the steel industry and the collapse in demand for manufactured steel and special steels. Their forecast that 40,000 jobs would be lost was well founded.

Three years before Bill Owen became president, Vernon Thornes was appointed secretary to the trades and labour council, moving from a similar post in Rotherham in January 1957. Born in Dewsbury, he had left the area in 1947 to become an organising lecturer with the National Council of Labour Colleges in West Wales. During his 27 years with the trades council he helped write its centenary history, and wrote pamphlets on William Dronfield and the Chartists. His working partnership with Bill Owen continued when the trade union and political groupings in the council parted company in 1973 on instructions from the Labour Party at national level. Bill remained as president of the trades council and simultaneously became chairman of the District Labour Party.

❝ The trades and labour councils were a survival of the Labour Representative Committee launched by the Trades Union Congress around 1900, but there were very few of them about, except in Wales. There was a high preponderance of trades union involvement in the trades council in Sheffield, and also in the Labour Party. This was partly the nature of the area. Sheffield has never had a very large commercial centre, but has been predominantly industrial. Consequently the only people apart from those whose political interests were awakened by the trades unions tended to be

With Councillor Harold Lambert in May 1969 when Bill fought off a serious threat from the Tory candidate for the Darnall ward.

Vernon Thornes

professional people. Sheffield had a university and FE colleges, and along with the secondary and comprehensive schools, these threw up a lot of people with a radical background, most of whom turned to the Labour Party in different ways.

But Sheffield was unique in one sense - the autonomy of the constituency party was all prevalent. I was never even invited to address a constituency party meeting in Attercliffe in the whole of my time there, and when I visited others it was only when they were seeking information or guidance. Park and Attercliffe constituencies had Sidney Dyson as joint agent and he was, of course, a prominent and influential alderman. Though he and I got on reasonably well, he was very much a man who safeguarded his own patch. It seemed to me that as long as things went reasonably well, why should I get involved just for the sake of getting involved? I've never believed in doing things if somebody else was already doing them well. So my activities were almost entirely centrally based.

The person I had most contact with at the beginning was the president, Joe Madin. He was a somewhat elder statesman when I met him, but he still worked at the city engineers department, one of the old time craft engineers, and he was very interested in the university. He was given a doctorate in his latter years and he was very proud of that because he always felt that it was as much a recognition of the movement as it was of Joe Madin.

I got to know Bill Owen when we wrote the centenary history. He became president when Joe Madin had a fall-out and stood down after an inquiry. Bill stayed as president until he stepped down about the same time as I retired. His last annual report was to the 1984 meeting, but he was not as active in the trades council in his latter days. I think he felt out of tune with some of the people who had come in.

When I first knew the trades council, it was dominated by manufacturing industries and unions - and I include in that service unions such as railways and buses. After I became secretary, we set our stall out to attract what used to be called the white collar workers. We got the Sheffield branch of NALGO and that was quite a prize because it was a very big organisation and it was worth a lot of money to us in affiliation fees. We managed to pick up all the teacher unions including the technical teachers, and we then picked up a number of ASTMS members who included university people and higher management. So we became a very representative body and must have nearly doubled our affiliated membership. I can remember we had in excess of 250 trade union branches and it would cover over 100,000 members.

As unemployment grew in the steel industry and the engineering industry it meant that the numbers affiliated from them reduced quite sharply, particularly from the iron and steel trades. This altered the balance, and the interests of the white collar workers became more predominant than those of the industrial workers. I did my best to make certain that they weren't overlooked, but that was not as easy as it sounds because you have to follow the wishes and the decisions of the majority. To some extent Bill was unhappy about these changes.

He always left a lot of the administrative work to me, but I tried to consult him as much as possible. He was much better as committee man than he was presiding over a big organisation. In his latter days he wasn't quite as patient with some of the younger people and some of them deliberately went out of their way to try and trip him up. I used to smile to myself when that happened because Bill's knowledge of chairmanship could have been improved on, and having taught chairmanship for the TUC on many occasions I knew a little bit about it.

He always used to start off by saying 'Oh no no no, we can't possibly do that!' And then having heard about four speakers, 'Well we might think about it', and if he felt he was in a minority of one he'd say 'Well, yes, I think we might manage to do that.'

The most awkward meetings were when we had close votes, and on one occasion there was a tie and he said to me 'What do we do next?' I said 'Take another vote', and lo and behold, there was a difference of two - so he wasn't put in the unfortunate position of having to say yes or no. Towards the end there were grumbles and suggestions about unseating him, but most of the people who had a chance were not prepared to stand.

Bill was a difficult person to get to know and you wouldn't get close to him easily. He had rather a dour and dry sense of humour that was typical of Sheffield people - they always keep a straight face when they are pulling your leg - but once I got used to it we got on reasonably well. I don't think he had a great many close personal friends. He wasn't a person to neighbour or invite people to his home. The only times I went to visit him was when he was ill and I visited his house two or three times to keep him in touch. I was at his wedding to Sheila, of course.

He didn't smoke and he didn't drink often, although he did have a passion for liqueurs and that surprised me. We used to go in the pub in the square next to Transport House - the Dove and Rainbow - after our main delegate meetings but it's not often he would he join us, and if he did it would be a soft drink most of the time.

His greatest strength was his background. There was no doubting his knowledge of the history of the movement. He used to make up his own mind - he didn't have to read a newspaper to be told what to think. He was a self-made man in that sense. He took advantage of libraries, he had a good library of his own, and he was familiar with all the radical writers and thinkers of the time. And of course he lived through a remarkable period himself. I remember him telling me that as a boy of about twelve he was on the steps of the Telegraph when they announced the 1926 local election results, the first time there was a Labour majority. Now there can't have been many youngsters who remembered being there on such an occasion, but Bill remembered it so vividly.

His major contribution to Sheffield was definitely in the field of education but it was education in the broadest sense. He never had any children but he still took an interest in primary, and an even greater interest in secondary education, and that was on top of his tremendous work in further and higher education, which included the University as well as the Polytechnic. **,,**

Jack Illingworth was vice-president of the trades and labour council to Bill Owen's president. He was Bill's deputy chairman at Shirecliffe College and sat alongside him again as a governor of Sheffield City Polytechnic. Full-time chairman of Firth Brown's shop stewards committee, and a member of the Plumbing Trades Union which later amalgamated with the electricians to form the EETPU, he also worked with Bill at the Confederation of Shipbuilding and Engineering Unions. Few contemporaries in the trade union movement knew and respected Bill's strengths better than Jack Illingworth, and few were more ready to tackle his weaknesses head on.

,, Bill knew the rule book by heart and he impressed me so much that if he seriously said something was a fact I accepted it. I crossed swords with him many, many, many times but we respected each other and he was a great friend of mine right up to the end. We never fell out, I couldn't fall out with Bill.

Jack Illingworth

The evening of the last prize giving ceremony of Shirecliffe College in March 1988.
L to R: Ron Stringer, Acting Vice-Principal, Shirecliffe College; Jack Hall, Principal, Shirecliffe College; Bill; Jack Illingworth, Governor, Shirecliffe College.

There was a lot of in-fighting on the executive of the trades and labour council with different factions that were antagonistic to Bill. They couldn't get their own way when they wanted a political or even a trade union decision to come out more strongly, and they would get on their high horses and shout what they were going to do, and they would probably take a majority of people with them within the council. And I can see Bill now standing up and saying 'You're not on. You cannot do that via our constitution, we're not allowed to do that,' and he knew that book off by heart and defeated them on many occasions.

But the in-fighting still went on and both Richard Caborn and I were asked to oppose Bill for the chairmanship, which we refused to do. Both of us could have taken that post off him without being clever about it at that time, so strong was the sway that was trying to get rid of Bill at that time - not for his lack of ability but for their own inability to go extreme left. I'm not saying he never did anything wrong, but in the main Bill was trying to do what he thought was the best for the movement as a whole, whether it was trades council or Labour group.

I remember my first Labour Party Conference in Blackpool when Bill, Vernon Thornes and I were delegates, and I was very much a new boy. I'd done quite a few trade union conferences but not been involved in the deep end of political issues, though I'd always been brought up politically.

Bill taught me what to look for, what to disregard, not to sit there for a full week and gobble the whole lot up, but to pick out not only the interesting bits but the bits that matter. We were having a cup of tea in a cafe at the back of the conference and Frank Cousins who was then a government minister, or on the way up, shouted 'How do Bill lad, hows tha' going on?' Frank Cousins sat down and Bill said 'Let me introduce you to one of my young colleagues, Jack Illingworth here' and immediately I was the topic of conversation. Bill and George Caborn always brought people on like that. They had that ability.

When we did cross swords we did it in the full knowledge that if I was critical of summat he was doing Bill would look at the position and perhaps take a couple of paces back - because if people like Jack and Richard were opposing him then perhaps he was getting a bit too inflexible. We'd have off the cuff meetings and come to a compromise on whatever issue it was. That was the pattern for a number of years.

One of the things we crossed swords over was the Reading System, which involved swelling the constituency with thousands of workers during an election campaign, and you fetched in all your known supporters by knocking right up to ten o'clock. Teams of workers knocked them up until that person got so fed up he'd go and vote. I was brought in to Bill's ward in Walkley to organise and spell out how the system worked, and I took over Bill's house.

Whoever is doing the Reading System has got to be in charge and nearly all the calls that particular day were for Jack Illingworth, and Jack Illingworth was very much in charge. I remember shoving Bill out of way and telling him to bugger off, I couldn't work with him hovering around. 'Either get summat done or go in park for t'day' and he took it and cleared off for a bit. Then we got a complaint from one of the schools where the presiding officer was not allowing our supporters to take their numbers within the school premises. It was a bad day, started to rain and I had told them to stand just inside ... not to get wet through. Anyway they got ordered out even though all the political parties were doing the same thing, so there was no scoring points.

I said 'Leave it with me, I'll get Councillor Owen to see the presiding officer.' I went upstairs and I told Bill about this and he stood there and was telling me how to do it, and I says 'Bill, I'm giving you a job. Now get off thi' bum and go and do it!' He said 'Ah, ah, right oh Jack!' and put his coat on. If you weren't careful Bill would be showing you the job, but as I said we never fell out because we could deal with each other on an acceptable basis. I respected him tremendously and I'm sure he did me.

When the city started to appoint school governors, Bill encouraged me to take the chairmanship of a special school for the mentally and physically handicapped, Norfolk Park. We did a tremendous amount of work both for the school itself and also for the council with the support of Ironmonger and Dyson. When the school was collecting money for a hydrotherapy pool, the Firth Brown workforce, about 5,000 of them, all put in £1 each and the company doubled it.

After that Bill and I never looked back. I became a governor at Shirecliffe College and became his vice chairman there. I also became vice president of the trades and labour council and Bill used to say he never had to look over his shoulder for somebody trying to remove him. He had somebody there who fought his corner, and when the trades council were nominating delegates for the Polytechnic he and I were governors for more than 20 years up to my retirement.

I protected Bill from everybody bar me. Nobody called Bill Owen anything without an argument from me - but I'd do it. I thought he should have packed it in earlier, but perhaps he knew better. He had no fall back. He didn't like gardening and he had no DIY sense whatsoever. In fact, one of the things that Bill admired about me was that I was a tradesman, and he wasn't. I remember seeing Bill before a meeting when he lived in the Rivelin Valley with his first wife, and Rivelin was a million miles away from where I lived on Gleadless Valley.

He caught me just before the meeting started and said 'Jack, I've got a problem at home. I can't turn me cold water off on the washbasin in the bathroom.' And of course being a plumber and a practical man I had visions of the cold water filling up the wash hand basin. He said 'I wondered if you'd come up and have a look at it after the meeting?' and I says 'Well if you think it'll last that long' - thinking of carpets getting wet and his wife sat downstairs and water dripping through ceiling. And he said 'No, no, no, it's not running out bad, it'll cope with that.'

After the meeting ended he jumped in my car and guided me to Den Bank, and his wife was sitting there. I went straight upstairs, listening for the pressure noise from the cold water tank, but the washbasin tap was just dripping, about one drip a second. I got hold of the tap and gave it a full quarter turn which stopped it. I swore at Bill. 'You've dragged me up here!' His finger came out and pointed to the H and C letters on the taps, and if you turned the tap right off, the C was not square. 'Ah!' he said, 'you can stop it like that, but look at C!' I said 'Bill, I'll bloody strangle you, you've ...' and he had a rare grin and we went downstairs and had a cup of tea. To this day I'm convinced I got him a lift home that night.

His greatest strength was his brain power. He wasn't briefed just for the occasion, he was briefed from leaving school. Sometimes at meetings, when raving left wingers jumped up and started trying to move things, he would quote the rule books from memory. And it wasn't only silly people. I can remember when George Caborn and I would be sitting together and we'd say 'You're wrong Bill, hold on a bit! We want to be doing so and so.' And old Bill would jump to his feet as the secretary and say 'George, I'm telling you, that resolution will get us nowhere' and a lot of people wanted us to continue with that resolution. But we would then take two steps away from it. I can see George, who guided me in all my industrial thinking, saying 'Bill's right, we are going a bit too far here.'

He was always right with me. Bill came up in the days of Ron Ironmonger and Sid Dyson and if you didn't know your rule book you were destroyed. These people didn't destroy Bill, they worked with him. You don't survive on a tightrope of pretending you know. They were people who suffered no fools and Bill was never accused of being a fool in the council chamber. Many a time laughed at - because Bill could be one of the most humorous people you'd ever come across, often when he wasn't trying to be. He could carry a meeting with a bit of humour coming into it, sometimes at his own expense, and he capitalised on it.

The full-time union officers in Sheffield would meet at a factory somewhere, might even have been right on the edges of Tinsley, and of course

Bill had no car. Nearly always he came with George Caborn. They travelled together a lot and George would say to him during the interval with employers, 'I've got to get straight off, no hanging about after meeting, no cups of tea.'

Bill, Chairman of Sheffield City Polytechnic's Governing Body, and John Stoddart, Principal, on the day the Polytechnic confirmed an Honorary Fellowship on Jack Illingworth (centre)

The end of the meeting arrived and George very much a man of his word jumps up and shouts 'Right, I'm off Bill, come on if you're coming!' and Bill stood up - and this is factual, although I wasn't there - looked round and said 'George, I'm having a lift with er ... Harry' and he picked his lift out. None of them knew anything about it, but he picked his lift out, and all the rest of the full-time officers fell about with laughing.

Of course as a full-time officer he could have had a car at any time he wanted. He had lessons, but he told me 'I can drive Jack, my tutor said I can drive. My problem is I just can't steer!'

He used to have a handyman doing jobs for him at home, including his garden, and Sheila one night got fed up striding over his feet stuck out, six o'clock at night in the summer, and said to him 'Why don't you go and do a bit of weeding?' And these are Bill's words, as Bill told it to me, and I can see his cheeky grin at the time, 'I'd been out about half an hour and this chap had come on duty to do his night's work and he says 'What the bloody hell tha doing, Bill, tha's pulling a row of carrots up there!' And Bill says to me 'Jack, I thought it were funny all weeds were growing in straight lines'. He knew he'd never be asked to get off his bum again and go in the garden.

In practical things he was hopeless. We used to be directors of Sheffield Forward and it was printed at Ripley. We used to have them delivered, but trades council couldn't afford it, so I used to fetch them with my car, and without exaggeration I'd fill the whole of my back seat with newspapers all bundled, front seat and the boot. The weight was tremendous, really far too much for a little car to carry, but I'd drive them down to the T & G. I'd chuck these bundles out on my own and the office foyer would be stacked nearly to the ceiling, and I was very mardy about it because I was on me own.

One night there was a Labour group executive and I'd arranged for some shop stewards to come, and Richard Caborn was coming, and we were going to parcel them, count them, and put them in collection order ready for the delegate meeting the following week.

Well Bill came down and said to me 'Eh, you can't leave that lot there!' I said 'Well Bill, if tha doesn't want them leaving there, thee shift 'em. I've just done my wack. I've just fetched all buggers from Ripley, and I've unloaded my car here. I'm coming back by six and we'll shift them then'. I arrived back at six and a few of them had been shifted into the upstairs conference room, so I put my fingers through two bundles and put them on my shoulder, up the stairs to the swing doors at top.

I kicked the first swing door open and dropped a bundle down to prop the door open and took the other bundle in. As I was coming back down, Bill was there helping, so I followed him up, and he'd just got his bundle down and was picking up the one that propped the door open.

'Don't touch that,' I shouted. 'Why?' he said. 'It's holding the door open, tha silly old bugger!' And then he said to me 'Eh, that's thinking as a tradesman that. We were coming up here and having to put the bundle down, open the door, and pick the bundle up again.' But that was Bill. **" "**

Portraits of a City Father

C H A P T E R   S I X
The Great and The Good

Although he had been fascinated by politics from the age of 12, and had been a member of the Independent Labour, Communist and Labour parties in turn, Bill Owen showed no interest in becoming a Sheffield city councillor until 1958, when he was already 44 years old. He stood in a by-election in the Darnall ward when the sitting councillor Mrs Alice Ives was elevated to the aldermanic bench and took his place in a council chamber dominated by some of the giants of the post-war local government scene.

The indomitable Alderman Mrs Grace Tebbutt was still deputy leader of the Labour Group but she was soon to take over as leader. Among the councillors were men and women who had made, or were about to make, names for themselves. They would be remembered with affection by Bill Owen in a series of interviews he gave shortly before he died - Albert Ballard, Sidney Dyson, Winifred Golding, Ron Ironmonger, Harold Lambert, Isidore Lewis, Hartley Marshall, Patience Sheard, and James "Sunny Jim" Sterland among them.

Grace Tebbutt was, in Bill Owen's opinion, "an outstanding woman who was brilliant as a leader, although the brains behind her was Jim Sterland - he would never oppose her, although he ought to have been leader himself." Born in Attercliffe, she became a councillor in 1929, the city's first alderman in 1934, the first socialist female Lord Mayor in 1949 and the first woman to speak at the Cutlers' Feast during her year in office. A Freeman of the City of Sheffield, she was made a Dame Commander of the British Empire in 1966, retired from politics a year later, and died in 1983 at the age of 90.

Chairman of the children's committee and a willing worker for many hospital and children's organisations, she also won Bill Owen's admiration for her campaign for more green space and recreation facilities when she was chairman of the parks committee.

Bill Owen was later to chair that committee himself and make his own contribution to opening up the parks to Sheffield people, but after his election he first became a member of the education and the housing committees. Later he added libraries, art galleries and museums, and parks. He was made an alderman in 1970 but enjoyed the privilege only until 1972 when the aldermanic bench was swept away in local government reorganisation. He was then chosen to represent his "home territory" in Walkley. Dorothy Whittington, secretary of the ward party remembered his delight: "He thought a lot about Darnall but when he came to Walkley he was so pleased because it was the area he had been born and brought up in."

Perhaps the only surprising aspect of Bill Owen's 34 year period as local councillor was that it did not begin sooner. He recalled in later years "It was Sidney Dyson, who was in the same union as me, who finally persuaded me to stand for the council in 1958. I had resisted until then. Dyson had outstanding ability, but he was very arrogant at times. He was a formidable debater and opponent but never bore malice."

Sidney Dyson was also a maverick, described as "forthright, audacious and controversial" during his year as Lord Mayor in 1970/71. Bill Owen believed he was a potential leader of the council who failed to attract enough backing to unite the Labour group behind him. Yet he was powerful enough to be tagged the "uncrowned King of Sheffield" by local journalists.

Born in 1910, the son of a miner, Dyson started work at 14 as a butcher's boy, and joined the Union of Journeyman Butchers, later becoming a member of the Transport and General Workers Union. He was elected councillor for Park ward in 1944, and when his ambitions turned towards Westminster in 1956 he was shortlisted for Sheffield Park constituency. Although he was not chosen, he agreed to be the electoral agent for the man who beat him to the nomination, Fred Mulley.

Sidney Dyson later admitted he felt some bitterness at his rejection, but he concentrated instead on local government, particularly on Sheffield's transport committee which he had chaired since 1954. Bill Owen wrote in an obituary in 1978 that Dyson had "transformed the undertaking into one of the finest in the country," even though confrontation over wages and conditions made him so unpopular that at one stage bus crews demanded his resignation, leading to a six-week long strike. He switched to the housing management committee in 1966, but controversy followed when he introduced the unpopular rent rebates scheme which many observers blamed for Labour's year in opposition after the loss of 12 seats in the 1968 election.

Bill Owen saw it differently: "Sid got blamed for it, but the whole of the Labour Group and the District Labour Party supported him at the time. They deny it, some of them, but it's true."

When Sidney Dyson died in March 1978, columnist Peter Harvey wrote in the Morning Telegraph: "Think of any political controversy there has been in Sheffield in the last 30 years and it is odds-on that Sidney Dyson was up to his neck in it. Whether it was air facilities, or pedestrian precincts, rent rebates, direct labour, press relations, local government reorganisation or - more than anything else - public transport, he was invariably at the heart of it.

"Some months after David Hopkinson left the editorship of the Morning Telegraph to become editor of the Birmingham Post, I met him and asked him what Birmingham City Council was like as a forum. It was all right, he said. It was progressive, lively. 'But it doesn't have a Sidney Dyson.' Neither do we now, more's the pity."

Wherever the fault lay for their short loss of popularity, the Labour group had time to re-think their policies during their year in the wilderness. In 1969, the Labour group leader, Ron Ironmonger, sent for Bill Owen. "He said I could continue as chair of the party if I wanted, but he would prefer me to become deputy chair of education to Peter Horton. I didn't specially want it, but obviously they wanted me to accept."

When Sir Ron chose to become the first leader of the new South Yorkshire county council in 1974, few Sheffield councillors were more aware of Sheffield's loss than Bill Owen, who had been impatient with Ironmonger's detractors four years earlier. "He was criticised for accepting a knighthood, but I always felt it was up to the individual. I have been asked on four separate occasions if I was interested in receiving a Queen's honour but I said 'What, Other Bugger's Efforts OBE - not me,'" Bill said.

Sir Ron confessed his decision had not been easy: "Being the kind of socialist I am, you are inclined to identify gongs and titles with the system you are trying to eradicate. But it is Sheffield's achievement which is being recognised and I have been lucky to be associated with that."

The son of a railway worker, Sir Ron's first job was in a non-union factory, Laycock Engineering, but he joined the AEU "very quietly indeed," and six years later he was a shop steward at Metrovick, which became part of General Electric. He was elected a city councillor for Tinsley in 1945 and served on a variety of committees. Made an alderman in 1962, a Freeman of Sheffield in 1979, he died at the age of 70 after suffering several strokes.

If Ron Ironmonger was, in the words of his contemporaries, "one of the best leaders" the Labour group ever had, and "one of the nicest men you could meet," Isidore Lewis was without question "the most respected authority on local government expenditure to sit in the Town Hall since the war." He handled the city's budget for 25 years, from 1952 to 1976, and although many colleagues considered him a right-wing socialist, his financial acumen was respected by all political groups on the council.

Born in Scarborough, he moved with his parents to Sheffield a few months later, attended Upperthorpe and Sharrow Lane schools and then the London School of Economics. He became a councillor for the former St Philips and

Cathedral wards in 1946, an alderman in 1956, and Lord Mayor in 1963. He was managing director of two cutlery and silverware companies from 1923 to 1969.

When "Izzy" Lewis eventually relinquished his expert hold on the city's purse strings in 1976, he talked openly about the loneliness of being chairman of the finance committee. "You always have to be nervous of outside contacts. Some of the negotiations we were involved in to acquire sites for redevelopments were very confidential and involved large sums of money. You can't go around chatting about things like that. Even among my colleagues on the council I could only discuss these matters in a very small circle."

Asked if his enforced aloofness made him unpopular, he showed no hesitation in replying "I have always said that the most you could expect was the respect of your colleagues." When he died in 1983 the tributes demonstrated that he had never lost it.

Jim Sterland, who outlived him by nearly a decade, was a remarkable character whose popularity was seldom questioned. In a council already rich in idiosyncratic but able men and women he was a major figure from 1937 until he retired in 1974. For 27 years from 1947 he was chairman of the town planning committee, guiding Sheffield through major changes after the war. He attracted laughter and some derision during his year as Lord Mayor in 1961 when he talked about making the city a conference and tourist centre. But by the 1980s, the council's publicity department had proved him right.

A Freeman of the City, 29 years a magistrate, and a director of Sheffield United football club, "Sunny Jim" Sterland lived up to his nickname in his "buoyant and friendly" approach to local government, but behind the easy-going manner there was an effective, keen mind. As Roy Hattersley said after Jim Sterland's death in March 1992 at the aged of 93: "He was one of the great men of the Labour Party, to whom Sheffield owes an incalculable debt."

Winifred Golding was one of the leading women councillors of the post-war era. Lord Mayor of Sheffield in 1977 when Bill Owen married his second wife, Sheila, Mrs Golding was among the guests at their wedding reception. Affectionately known as "Winnie", Mrs Golding was a councillor for 26 years, the last ten of them representing Heeley ward. She was chairman of social services for many years and deputy chairman of health.

Both she and her husband Arthur were Londoners but they settled in Sheffield after the war. Winnie Golding had joined the Labour Party as soon as she was old enough, and when she moved to Sheffield she began working for the party in Nether Edge, where she still lives.

"Bill Owen and I joined the council on the same day, but he was already well known as secretary of the trades and labour council," she recalled. "I don't think we were on a single committee together, but nevertheless he was a person for whom you felt greater respect the more you got to know him.

"It was always helpful to know he was behind you. His integrity, his honesty, soon became very apparent. It was unfortunate for him that his ideas were very sound and he took a full part in debates but he was not fluent. He was certainly a worker."

Among other women in public life about whom Bill Owen talked with respect and admiration in his later years was Patience Sheard - "She was an outstanding councillor, no question about that, and a very nice lady as well. She was famous for pushing the Clean Air Act through Sheffield."

In fact, Mrs Sheard achieved a great deal more in nearly 30 years as a councillor, although it was undoubtedly her determination and resilience in putting an end to Sheffield's almost perpetual pall of smoke and smog that made her a public figure. She represented the old Firth Park ward from 1945 until she became an alderman in 1958, and was later re-elected for Nether Shire ward. She was Lord Mayor in 1968, and retired from the council in 1984 to spend more time with her husband, Rowland. As chairman of the Health Committee of the Association of Municipal Corporations, Mrs Sheard made a wider impact on national affairs, serving also on advisory bodies to the Ministry of Health covering welfare, handicapped persons and mental health. She was a member of the Clean Air Council and of various other health organisations.

"I know people talk about me and Clean Air, but most of the work I did as chairman of Sheffield health committee was medical. We started the first home help service using permissive legislation, and year after year, right up to my leaving in 1974, we never did have a cut in it. And we were the first local authority in the country to set up a full blown consumer protection department," she pointed out.

When the Clean Air Act was introduced as a Private Member's Bill by Gerald Nabarro in 1958, it was permissive rather than mandatory, but Patience Sheard was chairman of the smoke control subcommittee and she realised the legislation was tailor-made for Sheffield, with its reputation as the dirtiest industrial city in Europe.

"We had heavy industry - specialised steels - which meant multiple processes burning coal, surrounded by densely populated housing. These were back to backs, built throughout the industrial revolution. We were the biggest coal burning city in the country and the smoke spread so that you couldn't see across the city. And you could only grow good plants in the south west.

"The difficulty was that other towns didn't do anything about clean air, particularly in the mining areas, because it posed a threat to coal. People's fires had to be converted to burn smokeless fuel or electricity or gas, with the local authority paying 30 per cent, the householder 30 per cent and government 40 per cent. We had to approach it in a planned way, through a series of smoke control zones working alongside industry. We started at the east end of Sheffield where all the heavy industry was located, then added a zone in the centre of the city, then a zone at the south west - following the direction of the wind, in fact, so that when a zone was completed, people could see the difference."

Patience Sheard was convinced that if the rolling programme could be sustained for three or four years it would become popular, making it difficult for government to withdraw financial support. She was right. Sheffield carried its programme through systematically and government money was made available to complete it.

When Mrs Sheard remembers Bill Owen, and the support he gave to the clean air campaign, it is with a reciprocal admiration: "He was a socialist of simple belief, and when I say simple I don't mean simplistic. He had a pure belief based on a real understanding of what politics meant. But he must also have been a very subtle political thinker. The fact that he could survive all those years in the trades and labour council, enrich its work, and survive various upheavals without trimming - because he was not a trimmer, nor was he a fence sitter - means that he must have been a subtle thinker.

"He was always very quiet, but though he never really said a lot he had an instinct for supporting the fundamentals, without causing offence to people who called themselves the true democrats and were nothing of the sort. I can't remember any clash between us in the thirty odd years I was there, because we each understood our function. He was naturally reserved, but not secretive or deceptive.

"At the crucial moment he supported people in things he believed, and he would never support something that was wrong. He was an invaluable ally when you wanted to do something that wasn't always popular, and of course many things were not popular, nothing innovative is, but he was powerful support because people listened to Bill Owen. He was an influential person, no doubt about that. He was actually a good man, and you can't say more than that. Not many people are truly good, certainly not in politics, and he was."

CHAPTER SEVEN
Building Unity

Althought Bill Owen's day-to-day work as a city councillor attracted little of the press attention which followed Sidney Dyson, Ron Ironmonger, Isidore Lewis or Patience Sheard, there were colleagues and contemporaries who knew the power of his influence behind the doors that were closed to the reporters. They sat alongside him in Labour group meetings, in District Labour Party meetings, and trades council meetings. They stumped the streets in local and national elections, and even when they had reached the House of Commons, old friends like Martin Flannery consulted and kept him informed.

Councillor Bill Jordan, Sheffield's Lord Mayor from May 1992 to May 1993, was vice-principal of Shirecliffe College, a post which precluded his standing for election to the city council. But within a couple of months of taking early retirement in March 1984 he was a member of the council, representing Manor for Labour.

He first came to Sheffield in 1948 when he was already active in the trade union movement, but he had little contact with Bill Owen before leaving Sheffield in 1957. It was not until 1972, when he was interviewed for the Shirecliffe College post, that he actually met him.

Bill Jordan

"He was chair of the interviewing committee and that interview underlined all I'd heard about him - that he was a person of not so very many words but had an enormous reputation. That reputation must have been based on something, and a lot of people have asked the same question - how was he at the centre of things when, on the face of it, he was not an especially good communicator?

The fact is he was influential. He was an intelligent person with a very retentive memory, which could be a positive advantage in a meeting - he could always remember the minutiae of previous meetings. I became a member of staff at Shirecliffe College and had a great deal of contact with him there. I was also active in the National Association of Teachers in Further and Higher Education, and within a short time I went on to the executive of the trades council, so I had much to do with Bill in that context as well. I also served with him on the South Yorkshire committee of the trade union movement.

Again we worked together in the Get Britain Out campaign of '75. Bill of course was chair of both the District Labour Party and the trades council at that time. He was very active in that campaign and Sheffield was the area, rightly or wrongly, that registered the greatest percentage 'against' vote. Those of us who were against Britain retaining its membership did not take that line because we were little Sheffielders, or Little Englanders for that matter. On the contrary, we embraced the principles of internationalism, but at the time we saw the Common Market as a narrow organisation which was 'a rich man's club.' That was Bill's view and mine. We believed Europe was more than just western Europe.

His great contribution to Shirecliffe - and to further education generally - was to ensure within the city council that FE got its share of resources. The centre of his thinking and campaigning was to ensure that people had adequate opportunities for training and further education. Although he himself left school early, he knew the value of education, and was as disappointed as I was that in Sheffield we didn't materially change the take-up rate of post-16 education over many years. We had a very high percentage of skilled people in this area and you would think from that base we'd have ensured this city would be atypical of northern cities, where the take-up rate is below the national average.

Bill belonged to an era when we had a great many trade union and political leaders who hadn't been to university but who nevertheless were intelligent and often very well read. He believed that if you were going to have good advocates for the cause they had to be educated. I don't think he had any single idea why people should avail themselves of education. He would say that people the world over stand a much better chance in life if they have a reasonable education. He would also know that if the bulk of the population were better educated then it would be much better informed about its democratic choices.

From time to time Bill entertained some of the great and the good of the trade union and Labour movement at his house - Vic Feather and Len Murray among them. When Neil Kinnock stood for the leadership of the Labour Party he stayed with the Owens overnight and I was there that night.

By the time I came on to the council, Bill was still very much respected. Many people would say he stayed too long but he was determined to die in harness. Although he might get a bit bored because he couldn't hear properly, he was respected for what he had done for the city and that was evident in the way others treated him. Everyone spoke well of him.

He could be very outspoken, and I could never understand why he was like that. By nature he was a kindly person, but he would sometimes blurt things out - I think it could have been a defence mechanism. It may have been a way of putting some people off their guard, he may have employed it as a weapon against some. Generally, he was constructive. He would check whether or not he was on the right lines by talking things over with people like George Caborn - he worked closely with him and they fed off each other.

He liked having power, but he also had integrity and I think that's important. Bill and others like him ensured there was a close liaison between the political and the trade union movements and I think it upset him when the Labour Party nationally insisted that the trades council became separated from the political movement. I also believe that Bill's insistence on the link between the unions and the political movement had a salutary effect on the level of honesty of Labour politics. The Labour Party has been in power well over 60 years in Sheffield, and when you've been in power for a long time there can be problems with maintaining dynamism and integrity. When you've been exercising power for a long time, you can quite easily forget about the democratic process. Bill was always a good influence.

I think he felt regret over the last few years of his life - regret about what was happening in local government, regret about what was happening to the trade union movement. I am sure that he regarded what was happening nationally and locally in politics as an aberration and out of keeping with our best traditions. However, he was optimistic to the end and died as he would have wished on active service for the cause of democratic socialism. **,, ,,**

Martin Flannery was Labour MP for Hillsborough for 18 years until he retired in 1992. Born in King James Street in 1918, he attended the Sacred Heart Catholic School in Hillsborough. His father was a Dublin fusilier who had been stationed in Hillsborough barracks and stayed on in Sheffield after marriage, working as a storeman at Vickers. During war service with the Scottish Borderers and the Royal Scots, Martin Flannery was wounded in Burma. After the war he became head teacher at Crookesmoor School, a member of the national executive of the National Union of Teachers, and a member of Sheffield education committee. He was president of the Hillsborough constituency Labour Party and vice president of the trades and labour council. He won Hillsborough in the February 1974 general election, when Bill Owen was his agent.

"" I was always political. I'm of the left, always have been, and so was Bill. During my 18 years in parliament he was one of my closest colleagues and comrades. If he wanted to talk to me he only had to walk from the next street, fifty yards away. When he was my agent he really understood every detail. He would lay out the agenda and steadily work through it, so I could get on with the political work, knowing that the planning was in safe hands. He was so well known throughout the entire trade union movement that when we feared we would not have sufficient money we always finished up with more than we needed.

Before I went to parliament, we were involved in a tremendous struggle on

Martin Flannery

the executive of the trades and labour council. Men like Joe Madin, who was the president, and Sid Dyson were on that executive and there was a struggle between the right and the left. In the late 50s it came to a boiling point when the bus drivers and conductors were locked out, literally in the middle of the night. I described it to the press at the time as 'the three o'clock knock' and in the worst tradition of the capitalist bosses. The strike lasted about six weeks with everybody walking to work or getting lifts.

In addition to the leadership given by the transport workers, Bill Owen struggled against the city council on behalf of the workers. People like Len Youle, president of Hillsborough Labour Party, and I were deeply involved in the strike, but Bill led it. It transformed the politics of the whole of South Yorkshire because it defeated the right wing of the Sheffield council and Labour Party. Bill became president of the trades and labour council when Joe Madin stepped down, and Sidney Dyson said he would never come near us again, and never did. In the subsequent elections for the executive the left won out and many right wing councillors did not stand again or were not selected by their local parties. Sheffield moved to the left, and when the county councils were created we had more councillors there than anybody else. This had a tremendous impact, and undoubtedly resulted in the cheap fares policy on the buses, which the people of Sheffield wanted and still want. I had to fight for that policy in parliament, first of all against the Labour Party who objected to it, and then against the Conservative Party who are still victimising Sheffield because of it.

What I loved about Bill was that, when it was lonely to be struggling against your own council, his integrity was complete, because he saw the justice of the transport workers' cause. He fought against some of his closest friends, and believe it or not, after the struggle was won, he was on an even keel with them, because they respected his integrity and his human dignity, as well as his immense loyalty to working people. Bill's attitude to the people who had been defeated in that strike was an example of non-sectarianism to all of us. There was bitterness, but not from Bill. It was vital after the strike that we build unity, and the greatest unifier among us was Bill Owen. We all helped, but he was the linch pin, holding the Labour Party and the trade union movement together. We need a lot more Bill Owens at the moment - at local level as well as at national level.

Bill was a stalwart and brilliant fighter, and his range of knowledge was tremendous. He was so sane and level that even people who were totally opposed to him on the council, in whatever party, were regularly won over to his viewpoint, especially because they knew he had a mass following in the city. He was no sectarian and he numbered among his friends people of all persuasions. He spoke with courtesy and knowledge to everybody.

He was Mr Labour, not just in Sheffield but in his beloved Walkley. Everybody in the streets knew him, and he walked round the area all the time, even after his heart attack, dealing with tiny problems and large problems. I used to go out on the doorstep in the local elections, always with Bill, because we were known. We knocked at doors and they'd say 'Come on in Bill, let's have a cup of tea'. When there were problems that other councillors found very knotty, people would ask to see Bill, and he was indefatigable. I hadn't a car and Bill hadn't a car, and we used to meet often at the bus stop at the top of the street. I used to say 'For God's sake Bill, rest, stop walking about', and as I looked from the bus I would often see him walking along Bole Hill Road or on South Road, at it again, disappearing down a street.

After we'd finished meetings - and he'd been in meetings all day - he would say 'You'll have to get off on your own tonight, Martin. I must go back to my office.' I'd say 'Bill, it's getting on for ten o'clock.' And he would say 'Nonetheless, I've not managed to do certain things and I've got to do them, so sorry old lad,' and he'd go into Transport House and he'd work for hours. I used to feel guilty I was going home.

One of the last things Bill said to me, was 'You're not retiring are you, Martin?' I says 'I am, Bill. I'm in my seventies.' 'Now stop that nonsense' he says 'you shouldn't be retiring, that's all I've got to say!' **,,**

Mike Bower, leader of Sheffield City Council, has been an engineer, journalist, trade union official and, since 1981, business organiser of Sheffield Co-operative Development Group. Born in Colwyn Bay, he came to Sheffield in 1965 to work as a reporter on the Morning Telegraph before moving to The Star as labour correspondent. From 1977 to 1981 he was northern organiser of the National Union of Journalists. First elected to the city council in the Intake ward, he now represents Netherthorpe. He has been chairman of the education committee and Labour Group secretary. Elected leader of the Labour Group in May 1992 he now chairs the policy and personnel committees.

Mike Bower

❝ I got to know Bill partly through my job as a journalist but more as an NUJ delegate to the trades council when I was a young firebrand and he was grey-haired 'FatherTime' in the chair, always pretty firm with people like me, but tolerant. He was never insulting or particularly aggressive, but he was quite good at putting people in their places. And, of course, he had the offices next door to Sheffield Newspapers and they used to be our strike headquarters when the NUJ was in dispute.

He knew that I was a journalist trade unionist, but it was the trade union part of my activities at Sheffield Newspapers that he seemed more interested in. He had responsibility for Sheffield Newspapers at one time because his members were van drivers there, and I remember him telling me stories about how, during the war, they used to have to find employees for Sheffield Newspapers because it was regarded as an essential service. He knew a bit about Sheffield Newspapers, and he was keen on the fact that Sheffield Newspapers' journalists were more actively unionised when I was there than they had been in the immediate past.

I think he always saw me as being a young upstart, even in the last few years when I was in 'mellow middle age'. He was much older than me and he got more and more cantankerous as he got older and deafer, though he played the deaf old man bit up when he wanted to, he was quite cute about it. I was much less tolerant of him than he was of me. I could be quite critical of this 'old fashioned old man' as I saw him when I was in my late twenties, early thirties. But at a meeting when there might be disagreement about an issue, I always saw him as - well, what he was - a stalwart of the Labour movement in Sheffield who had a lot of knowledge, a lot of experience, and sound judgement based on that.

He was part of the old school, like the Sidney Dysons, the Ron Ironmongers, and the other giants of the local authority, but he wasn't part of them in quite the same way, because he had a very important job with the T&G and he seemed effectively to split his time between those. The astonishing thing about Bill, which I didn't really become aware of until I was asked to speak at his funeral and did research for it, was that he was not only involved in all sorts of things, he was *actively* involved in all sorts of things. There are a hell of a lot of people in public life who 'collect' places on committees or chairmanships, and don't do anything with them. And there's another group of people who limit themselves to a particular thing which they involve themselves in totally. Bill somehow managed to do a lot of things across an enormously wide spectrum and knew what was going on in all of them. He was never just a figurehead chairman. It was astonishing that he could sustain such a wide range over such a long period.

I'm sure he didn't see a distinction in his politics between his local authority and his trade union activities. They were all part of the same political work. But he managed to keep a balance between them. People listened to what he had to say, partly because he wasn't a full-time councillor. He was involved with working people as part of his daily life, and also had the authority of the District Labour Party, which he chaired, and of the trades council, which he chaired. He had enormous authority because of the many positions he held and also because he knew so much about what had happened in the past.

He was never dismissed as an old buffer, even when he was quite elderly and hard of hearing. Sometimes people were amused by the fact that he would talk so loudly when he was supposed to be whispering to somebody - but that was a product of being deaf, and he took their amusement in good part. He'd be in some quiet bit of the Labour Group and he'd turn to somebody and try to whisper something and it would come out as a shout 'Pass me that paper over there.' But his views were never regarded as being out of date. Despite having been around for so long, he was still up with what was going on. He was very interested all his life in young people, and he still had a rapport with young people. The same was true of councillors - he was very careful with members of the council, very encouraging, and he helped people along. He was very generous with his experience, sharing his knowledge and not in a condescending way. He was a good man in all senses of the word.

It's tempting to say higher education when you talk about his greatest achievement - the establishment of the FE colleges and the establishment and progress of the Polytechnic are the most tangible legacy. But I think Bill Owen's most significant contribution to Sheffield was that he held the Labour movement together, and until the trades council and the Labour Party were forced to separate by slavish bureaucracy from Labour Party head office, he kept the trade union movement and the Labour Party together, and that coherence and co-operation was very unusual. Bill was acceptable to the Communist left who were dominant in trades councils in areas like Sheffield, and also acceptable to the right wing of the Labour Party. Among other things this allowed the Labour Party to keep control of the city council without many ups and downs, and certainly without the dreadful in-fighting that went on in places like Liverpool and Birmingham and Leeds, where the trades council and the Labour Party were at each other's throats. And he sustained it over a very long period.

He created a stability which allowed long term planning and progress to be made across the city. That's a remarkable achievement and I don't know any other individual who could have done it. He didn't do it entirely by himself, but there aren't many other people who could have been so - I don't want to say 'clever', because he never gave the impression of being clever - he was so sound and trustworthy and straight. He was never plodding. He was sharp at recognising which way to move and on occasions when not to move. He wouldn't have been able to achieve what he did in further and higher education unless we'd had that sort of stability. **"**

CHAPTER EIGHT
A Real Local Councillor

T hrough three decades, from 1958 to 1992, Bill Owen was linked
indissolubly in most people's minds with further education, the trade
union movement and the trades council. His life revolved around the
big, if not always exciting, issues. Yet the people of Walkley can testify to the
time he spent walking around his local streets, talking to them, picking up the
gossip and the inevitable complaints. He seemed to find time for the little
things that loomed large in the lives of his neighbours in Walkley. Requests for
clearer numbering on old people's flats or repairs to a dangerous doorstep
were not overlooked as he worked long hours to prevent an industrial dispute,
help find accommodation for Chilean refugees or argue the case in council for
expansion of Sheffield Polytechnic.

Within months of becoming chairman of the parks committee he had
pushed through a resolution to remove "Don't walk on the grass" signs from
the city's parks. And he fought a constant battle to prevent cruelty to animals,
at least within the city's boundaries where the council had sufficient clout.
Conservative ex-councillor Pat Santhouse, Councillor Jean Cromar and
Blanche Flannery remember Bill Owen's other achievements, smaller, more
local, but no less important in any assessment of his legacy to Sheffield.

Pat Santhouse was elected to Sheffield City Council in 1966 and
represented Dore for 25 years until she retired in 1991. Born in Sheffield, she
was educated at High Storrs and worked as a GPO telephonist before
becoming a medical secretary. She married John Davey in 1980.

" I think I was probably the first working class Tory on the council. The odd thing was I was put on to the transport committee - a horrible committee for a woman at that time - and I still think it was because I was the only Conservative who supported the use of buses. I hadn't a car at that time, I couldn't even drive. I was also put on typical women's committees - social care and children's - and education. They tend to put new councillors on education because they don't realise what work is involved. But I quite enjoyed it after the first six months and I stayed on it for the rest of my time on council.

Pat Santhouse

Bill Owen was on education when I started, and for a while he was deputy chairman. He always believed the opposition had a role to play and he made certain that Conservatives were represented on all areas of education including meeting with the unions. Now that made him quite unpopular with the unions at one stage, but he insisted and it gave someone like me a wonderful insight into union relationships. That is something a lot of people don't realise, how fair Bill was over that.

Bill had a white miniature poodle when I first knew him and he used to take it for a walk everywhere with him, apart from actual committee or council meetings, and I've always been good with dogs. They like me, I like them, and I used to make quite a fuss of this poodle and it liked me. After I'd been on the council about a year Bill proposed a notice of motion, possibly on hare coursing, and he asked me if I would second it. I said I would, but I didn't realise the politics of it at that time - I should have asked the group first. They weren't very pleased but they gave grudging consent when it was too late. Bill was not terribly popular with his own group for asking me but we both had consciences and we both felt very strongly about certain aspects of the way in this country we treat animals. So unpopularity or popularity aside, we kept the pressure up and over the 24 years we had notices of motion on just about every aspect of animal cruelty.

We also got fox hunting banned on all land owned by the council. And Bill must have been in the same boat as myself - we were threatened by people anonymously over it. But Bill's attitude throughout everything was that it didn't matter how popular a thing was, if it was morally wrong it was wrong. He was ready to stand up against any of the threats that people wanted to make against him. Circuses with performing animals were banned on city council land. Again that was Bill's baby assisted by myself and again popularity was not the order of the day. Quite a number of the bigger circuses objected and council has had to stick pretty firmly to its views because some of the performing animal people have tried various ways of getting round the ban.

Goldfish as prizes at fairgrounds have been banned in Sheffield thanks to Bill and he has drawn to people's attention many examples of general cruelty - cruelty involved in shipping live cattle and other animals to the Continent.

Somewhere among Bill's papers is a list of everything that has been done. He read it out at my last council meeting when we reversed the usual procedure and I put down a notice of motion which he seconded. Even I was amazed. He'd gone through all the things that we'd done together in the council, and it was a very long list.

Bill wasn't stupid or sentimental about animals. He had a strong sense of what was right and what was wrong, and he was determined as far as he could to make the world a better place for animals as well as human beings. He wasn't a vegetarian. His attitude was that we were entitled to use animals, but we were not entitled to abuse them. Using animals to work for us or even as food was okay so long as one was humane. Using them for one's amusement was certainly not on.

He was a very sincere person. When he was speaking on something he really believed in, his sincerity shone out. I believe he changed the minds of a lot of people about what was cruel and what was acceptable. I don't think that Bill would have had a great deal of time for the animal liberation people. His views were very similar to mine - what one did had to be within the law. You had to use persuasion, and these people may be well meaning but they do far more harm than good. They tar people like Bill and I with the same brush - as being a bit loony.

If Bill had lived I believe he would have gone on to fishing. One of Bill's most famous comments was when my husband John said to him 'Well you know, half the population goes fishing.' And Bill replied 'Well if 50 million people do it, it still doesn't make it right.' I don't know what Bill's religious views were but even if he was an atheist there will be an awful lot of animals waiting for him on the other side.

Our relationship was very close, because I think Bill had a great regard for me as a person. I certainly had a great regard for him. He was a wonderful person. But on many matters we opposed each other in council vociferously. We opposed each other in committee vociferously. I think this is something that the new councillors don't appreciate as much as the older ones did - that you can disagree with somebody politically but you can still appreciate them as a person. That was the kind of friendship between Bill and myself and between myself and a number of senior Labour people. There were many things I disagreed with Bill Owen about and we would go at it hammer and tongs. In the latter years Bill liked to mix it with his own group and in education committees we would egg each other on. That's one of the privileges of being a senior statesman in Sheffield!

But as a general politician I think Sheffield has lost one of its greatest sons. A lot of the newer Labour councillors thought of him as a bit of an old buffer. They didn't realise the knowledge that was there and they came unstuck. He realised they had to learn and he meant them no harm most of the time. Bill had mixed with the greats of the Labour Party. 99

Blanche Flannery met Bill Owen in the late 1930s when he worked in the Left Bookshop, but it was not until 1972, when she became an APEX delegate to the trades council, that she worked with him politically. She was elected almost immediately to the executive, and then became a vice president. She worked as a secretary in the ASTMS and UCAT offices in Sheffield and was also Martin Flannery's secretary when her husband was a member of parliament.

Blanche Flannery

❝ I remember doing a little tribute to Bill when I was vice president of trades council and he was president, and one of the things I said was that he was very knowledgeable and wise - because he had a wise attitude, not knowing or cocky in any way. He really made you feel that he knew what he was talking about, without being domineering about it. And that was good for a woman, because I was the only woman on an executive of twelve for many years.

We argued of course. But the thing that I always admired about Bill was that he would argue for his point of view and then democratically accept the decision of the majority, and work just as hard for that as he would for his own point of view. Any arguments we had we overcame, because we came to a democratic agreement.

I was also on the board at Northern College with him as a trade union representative so I saw him in action. Then he became chair of Rivelin governors and I was vice chair, so we worked very closely together again. He took on a lot but he was disciplined and conscientious about the jobs that he did. He knew that if he agreed to be chair of anything, or if he took on any other responsibility, it would be another task to add to his already heavy load. But he did it.

He was a real local councillor, was Bill. Travelling up and down on the bus, quite a lot people come to you with their problems, and you could always pass them on to Bill. I've been on the bus, sitting with Bill, and people have sat down in front of us and said 'Nobody's been to see about that pavement' and Bill would say 'I've got it on the list, don't worry.'

And there were those maisonettes on Bole Hill Road, with elderly people living in them. Ambulances were constantly arriving there, but the numbers of the flats weren't obvious, so the drivers had to go inside and look at the list to

Local campaigner Bill delivers a petition to the Chairman of the Planning Committee

see if they had the right block. I was at the bus stop with Bill, and somebody said 'Nowt's been done yet about those numbers up there' and in less than a fortnight they were done - the numbers are now on the front. He must have gone into the department in the Town Hall and handled it straight away. **" "**

Jean Cromar joined Bill Owen as a councillor for Walkley in May 1987, replacing Alan Billings who had left Sheffield. She had moved from Cambridge to Sheffield 12 years before, working in an accountant's office for five years before studying economic and social history and politics as a mature student at the University of Sheffield. From 1984 to 1989 she worked for Bob Cryer, the Euro MP for Sheffield .

" My friendship with Bill really grew from October 1986 when I was selected to fight Walkley, and Bill and I stood as the two Labour candidates. He was very supportive. I had joined the Labour Party in 1970, held various positions within my own ward, Sharrow, and had been very active politically, working in campaigns throughout Sheffield. Bill said he was pleased when I stood for Walkley, and he was a great help.

Jean Cromar

One of Bill's advantages was that he didn't drive, so he walked everywhere round Walkley, and therefore he knew an enormous number of people, and he knew the area so well that he would pick up things on his travels. Not driving was a positive thing as far as Bill was concerned - waiting at the bus stop he would chat away to people and he had his ear to the ground about what people were thinking locally. He also used to pop in regularly to the lunch club which his wife Sheila ran, and he used to have his calls en route, various ports of call where he could just pop in if he wanted a cup of tea or wanted to rest his feet. He was very well respected in Walkley.

I got on with him very well, and in the last few years I was probably as close to him as anybody on the Labour Group. We could speak to each other quite frankly and I think we had a mutual respect for each other. We hold three surgeries a month in Walkley and the ward is unusual because at local election times they've always talked about 'the Walkley team' - 'these are your councillors, and this is the new councillor joining the team' - so it had been tradition in Walkley for all three councillors to attend all the surgeries. One of our surgeries is at Stannington on a Friday and quite often we didn't have any visitors at all, and Bill would spend an hour just talking to me and recounting various things from the past, about his childhood and about how his father was agent for the Tory MP in Hallam. He would tell me how he used to go out with his mother and take the soap box, because his mother was very active in the Co-operative movement.

He was very unhappy about the erosion of local democracy by the Tory Party, and he also had concerns about the Labour Party. Bill was a very disciplined politician and he told me that he never asked for positions in the party or in the Labour Group, but if ever he was asked to do something he did it. He believed in team work and he was very concerned about some of the things that were happening in the Labour Group. He would speak up on issues regarding Walkley, and one of the things that he was very annoyed about was when the council went on to a two-monthly cycle of meetings instead of one month, because he thought that made us less accountable. He hadn't realised it had gone through, because Bill was very deaf in his last years and he would sometimes miss things. One of the issues he was very angry about was the closure of Roscoe Bank School and I can remember him standing up in group and saying 'You'll be losing Walkley if you close Roscoe Bank School.' We did lose Walkley, but I think there were other issues.

A real local councillor - at party HQ

Another big interest was libraries, and he was very supportive of Walkley Library, which is a Carnegie Trust library. When he was recuperating after his heart attack, he used to walk to the library, read a few books and then walk back home again. When it was under threat of closure he tried to find out if there was anything in the Trust which would prevent closure - and that was only a couple of days before he died. There were a lot of public consultation meetings after Bill died, and in fact we didn't close any libraries in that round, but their opening hours were reduced.

Bill believed in accountability very strongly, and if decisions were taken that he didn't agree with, he would still go along with them, he would never try to undermine anybody. I think that was partly because he was in the Communist Party for ten years and was used to their discipline and trade union discipline. Quite a lot of members on Group now have never had that trade union discipline. But he would also fight for something. It was Bill who argued very strongly that I should be a governor of the Poly and of Northern College because he felt there should be more female participation - but he also told me 'If you're on, you'll be able to give me a lift to all the meetings!' That was his sense of humour.

The Northern College had planned to make a presentation to Bill on the morning he died. Sheila phoned me up that morning and I immediately phoned the college because I knew a meeting was going to be held. The principal, Bob Fryer, suggested at the meeting that when the library was restored it might be fitting if it was named after Bill.

My warmest memories of the last few years will be sitting chatting about the past and about bringing Bill up to date with what was going on - things he might have missed in group because of his hearing - not necessarily gossip but just being kept informed. He was always very welcoming, and he liked me to go in for a cup of tea or coffee, or pick him up a bit earlier for a chat. I think Bill had an awful lot of acquaintances, but I'm not sure how many close friends he had that he could talk to.

He did tell me one thing which I found very touching. We had got on to the council together and I had to come up for re-election the following year. My own ward where I live approached me because they knew I was on the panel and asked if I would be prepared to be nominated for Sharrow Ward. But I said no, because I'd only just been elected for Walkley and I felt I should carry on. Bill heard about this and said 'I quite understand if you want to stand in Sharrow because it's a safe seat, but I'll be very sad to lose such a good comrade and friend.' That meant a lot to me. ""

C H A P T E R   N I N E
Education
For All

Bill Owen's growing influence and reputation in Sheffield was inseparable from the rapid expansion of further education in the city between 1960 and 1992. Within a few days of Labour's return to power in 1969, after a year of Conservative rule, he was asked by the group's leader, Councillor Ron Ironmonger, to become deputy chairman of the education committee. He accepted immediately and became part of a strong team with the new chairman, Councillor Peter Horton, and the chief education officer, Michael Harrison.

Chairman of the further education, careers, and youth and adult subcommittees, Bill was also chairman of the governors of Sheffield City Polytechnic for 21 years and deputy chairman for another seven. He headed the governing boards of Granville College for 26 years, Shirecliffe College for 23 years, and Stannington College for one year. He was chairman of Myers Grove Comprehensive school, King Edward VII School, Walkley Infants and Rivelin First and Middle School for various periods, a governor of Loxley College and Sheffield local education authority representative on the Northern College board.

Not surprisingly, education was his theme when he was installed as Lord Mayor in May 1980. He argued that Sheffield could be proud of its education service and its success rate in public examinations, its university, polytechnic and colleges. But had the city done enough to encourage young people to use its excellent education services to the full?

"Sport for all is an excellent aim, but education for all is an even better target," he said. "The city must make a conscious and deliberate decision to produce a social climate which places much greater importance upon continuing education for all than has been the case so far."

Determined to look forward rather than back, Bill Owen had not forgotten the impressive advances made by Sheffield's education system in the previous decades, or the national reputation it had already begun to earn when Alderman Albert Ballard had been chairman of the education committee.

Co-opted as a member of the committee in 1926, when Labour first took control of the council, Albert Ballard remained a member for over 40 years, and was its chairman for 14 of them. He was elected councillor for Manor ward in 1942 and was elevated to the aldermanic bench in 1952. His honorary law degree from the University of Sheffield in 1959 was largely recognition of his work in education, which his deputy chairman Chris Price, Peter Horton and others were able to develop into a practical scheme for the introduction of comprehensive education in 1969.

The parallels between his life and Bill Owen's were obvious. He had left school at 13, studied with the Workers Educational Association, read widely from books he picked up for a penny each, and believed strongly in cutting the number of school examinations to the minimum. "So far as I can remember, I have taken only two examinations in my life," he said.

A parliamentary agent for the Hillsborough division, he was also chairman of the United Sheffield Hospitals from 1948 to 1963, and was Lord Mayor in 1957. He founded Sheffield Cooperative Party Ramblers club in 1921.

Alderman Ballard was still chairman of the education committee when Michael Harrison joined the authority as deputy chief education officer in January 1965. Appointed chief education officer two years later, Michael Harrison had moved through various ranks of assistant education officer in Cumberland, and before that had worked in the West Riding under Alec Clegg.

By the time he retired in May 1985, Sheffield had become "a hard driving education authority, always in the eye of the nation." He replaced an old pyramid system of management with a matrix model of management which put policy, leadership and development in the hands of professional education officers. Business management was made the responsibility of career local government officers, and field and intelligence work was to be carried out by advisers, education welfare officers, psychologists and careers officers. Initiative and responsibility was spread through the department, and Michael Harrison was "no longer the chap who sat at the top of the pyramid but the spider in the middle of the web."

Michael Harrison

"One of the reasons for Sheffield education's national reputation was the morale of the people working in the system.

It began to be known that we were an adventurous authority, full of go, and that meant bright people would be on the list of candidates for the top jobs. I was always in on these appointments because the quality of the leadership throughout the system was absolutely vital. We started ascending a spiral of virtue. Good leaders of schools and colleges brought in good heads of departments and good subject specialists. Sheffield became one of the places to work if you wanted to make it in education.

The city council wanted to be in front, they wanted to be known for their excellence of service. The community was a very well informed community. I remember when I came to Sheffield, Albert Ballard asked me 'Won't you find it very difficult to come from a county existence to a city existence?' And I said 'No sir, I don't think so, the principles are the same. The communications are easier, we should be able to do it better in a city than in a county,' and I've always believed that.

By the time I retired, one heard oneself saying 'If Sheffield can't do it well, nobody can do it well,' because of our special internal homogeneity.

Peter Horton and Bill Owen were very much a part of that in the way they expressed the city's social and educational aspirations. They were one with the city. Bill came from that dedicated generation of Labour Party people who had a deep seated belief in the virtues of education and what it could do for communities and the country. Quite rightly, he lived the belief through to the end of his life. He probably found the youth and community side particularly rewarding because it brought him close to community development. He was not an expert educationalist as Peter Horton was. He was a social educationalist, and his love for the further education side was very much linked to providing opportunity for people in work.

I worked very closely with Peter Horton. When I got the chief's job in 1967, Peter and I were 'starters' together, and there was a symbiotic relationship which went on until Peter stood down. He and I spent a lot of time together talking about developments. He came in as the ingenue, imported by Ron Ironmonger and Sidney Dyson as 'the lad' who would do the then policy group's bidding, those great iron aldermen of that generation. Peter turned out to be his own man and ran the education policy of the city because he knew the education world, he knew the game.

I talked less with Bill. He was a dry man, a man of few words. I got on with him very well but not on any intimate level, not as I would with Peter Horton, because we unburdened to each other a lot. But Bill knew that I knew he was the salt of the earth. He also knew that I was an education developer and my heart was in it. He understood that we were part of the same team. I was often surprised how warmly he spoke of me in unexpected circumstances, which must mean that he valued the kind of support I was giving him.

He had very firm views of his own about further education and youth and community, but at the same time he was willing to defer in questions of professional appointment or professional opinion. Since that was always given by me and senior colleagues with impartiality and integrity, he accepted it. There was very little conflict, though if he didn't agree with you 100 per cent over an issue he might become a bit mulish, dig his heels in and go quiet. But usually after a period of argument and debate he would come round.

If he had a fault, it was that he was a bit soft on the union side and sometimes gave away more than we advised. The result was that we tended to pay at the top of any bracket of discretion, and it was rather difficult to pull back from that when things got tight financially. But one of the good things about Sheffield was the consultative machinery we had with the teachers. Because we all knew each other well we could talk seriously about the deployment of resources. Peter Horton didn't mince words - if resources were to go in such and such a direction they couldn't go in the other. He invited people to exercise their judgement, so it was a mature and civilised kind of consultative atmosphere, and Bill was as much part of that as anybody else.

I'm sure Peter Horton couldn't have carried the burden alone, or with a lesser person than Bill Owen. The weight of the Polytechnic business and the FE college business and the subcommittee business was so great that it really needed a Bill Owen to hold it together. The fact that he was always there at the centre of it meant that people saw a unity - and that was very important for the name of the authority and for its reputation. Peter and Bill were foils to each other, they complemented each other well.

Peter's genius was to make a contract with the policy committee and the policy leaders of the Labour Group : if you keep the resources coming I will deliver you an education service which will be run as effectively as we can make it. When the hard days of financial constraints came along and youth unemployment increased, he and his successor Mike Bower carried the tertiary revolution through with closure of the minimum number of secondary schools and the most effective use of school places. **"**

Peter Horton's credentials for succeeding Albert Ballard in 1967 were already established when he was elected to the council in 1962 to represent Castle Ward. He grew up at South Wingfield in Derbyshire, won an 11 plus pass place at Swanwick Hall Grammar School at his second attempt, studied at Manchester University and was then employed on war work at what is now GEC Rugby. After the war he became a teacher at New Mills Grammar

School in Derbyshire, and in 1951 moved to Sheffield to be head of biology at Woodhouse Grammar School in the West Riding. The school later became a comprehensive and was moved to Aston, but it was still under the West Riding education authority when he became a council member.

He was chairman of the education committee from 1967, with a break of only one year in 1968/69, and almost immediately became a close friend of Bill Owen. He was best man at Bill's marriage to his second wife Sheila on September 3 1977.

" I got to know Bill through the trades and labour council. He was already a member of Sheffield City Council when I was elected in 1962 and even then was showing great interest both in education and in recreation, libraries and arts. Bill was a prominent member of the education committee and a great supporter of comprehensive education, which was something that I had been advocating since 1955.

Peter Horton

The Socialist Education Association had been formed in 1959 with people like Chris Price, Bill Owen, Martin Flannery, Joe Albaya and one or two others, and we set about educating the Labour and trade union movement about the need to get rid of the 11 plus. The first breakthrough in Sheffield was the creation of Myers Grove in the late '50s - our first comprehensive school - which was supported by Roy Hattersley, his mother Councillor Enid Hattersley and his father, Roy senior.

Bill had also become involved in further education, both in the College of Technology and College of Art as they were then called, and in developing the further education colleges. These developments were gathering speed as part of a plan developed after the 1944 Education Act had suggested that ten county colleges - or FE colleges as they became known - would be developed in Sheffield.

By the mid-60s there were two - Granville and Shirecliffe - and then Stannington and Richmond were built. The next one was scheduled for Dore, but once I became the chair of education in 1967, Bill and I moved it to become the 'cross-the-road' half of Granville. We felt that ten colleges were too many for Sheffield.

I was chairman for only one year and then the Tories took over for one year. When we regained power, I became chair again and Bill Owen was asked to be deputy of education to form a solid base with me. He would have had the opportunity of being chair of recreation and probably libraries and arts, which were two of his loves, but he sacrificed these to be my deputy, and particularly to look after further education - both the colleges and what soon became the Polytechnic, which expanded and eventually incorporated City Training College and Totley Training College.

Bill was heavily involved in these developments and in the colleges, where he seemed to be the chair of most of them at one time. Once he took up something he gave it all he'd got and it was with difficulty that he could be persuaded to give it up. He was also very interested in adult education and the WEA and in youth activities. He wasn't a good speaker although I think he improved quite a bit because he began to sit on so many platforms. But it was noticeable at the beginning and people perhaps thought he wasn't well read, but of course it was the exact opposite. It was a handicap, but he was a power behind the scenes in so many ways and enjoyed that role.

We got on well. There were differences between us, but it was a good combination of a younger person who was involved in schools education and an older person who hadn't had much schooling but had educated himself in public libraries and through WEA. Like many of the pioneers of the 30s, Bill had been grateful for a second chance of getting an education when school elementary education finished at 14 for the vast majority. So it's not surprising that he was the instigator from Sheffield of the Northern College. When the steering group was set up by Sheffield, Barnsley, Rotherham and Doncaster, I became its chair - I suppose Bill felt that the chair of education in Sheffield could command the steering group more easily than he could. But having set it up, Bill again became totally immersed in it and was very much respected by the lecturers, by the other districts, and by the unions.

I think we complemented one another because of our background and difference in ages. We weren't exactly rivals, as we might have been if we were the same age. He had the backing of the trades and labour council and the Labour movement, so if he agreed with something I was aiming for I knew I could expect the backing to carry it out - like comprehensive education.

Before we went into opposition in 1968/9, for instance, school governors in Sheffield and in most other cities were a bit of a laughing stock. There weren't any in primary schools and one group of governors, mostly members of education committees, looked after six secondary schools. What happened at meetings was that the six head teachers sat in a corridor outside and were called in for ten minutes one by one. It was very undignified.

My experience had been in Derbyshire and the West Riding where schools had governing bodies made up of people from different areas of interest and from different villages. I'd seen them in action and felt we should have governors like this for every school. Colleges already had democratic boards of governors which included people from commerce and industry. Bill knew this and was very supportive of the idea of a set of governors for every school.

During our year in opposition we suggested the idea of teacher governors and parent governors. The chief criticism of our system and of that across the country was the governors were representative but they didn't seem to have any powers. It's ironic that further developments have given governors perhaps more powers than they really want! But we were one of the pioneers in Sheffield.

Not everybody agreed with us, because it meant giving proportionate representation to the opposition, and it meant we could even lose control of the chairs of some of the schools. But Bill was a power in getting it through despite opposition in the Labour movement. We had to negotiate with the Tories in power at the time and they agreed that whoever gained power in 1969 would carry this out. We agreed that the number of Labour governors to Tory to Liberal would be in exact proportion to the seats in the council chamber.

Later in the 1970s, Bill supported moves towards greater integration of those with handicaps and he was certainly an early advocate of what we would now call tertiary colleges. He disliked sixth form colleges because they were simply for groups of 16-19s mainly studying A levels. He felt this work should be done within a broader spectrum - within FE colleges so that students could mix an A level with maybe a practical subject for City & Guilds. In the 70s we had ended up with some schools with sixth forms, some without, and FE colleges effectively offered little in the way of A levels. After a brief, and perhaps lamentable, move to give every school a sixth form we were convinced we should move to a different system of tertiary colleges.

That didn't take place until 1987 and I think Bill felt we should have made a start in the early 70s, while I felt that there wasn't the support necessary for it among the teaching profession at that time.

I probably regret that now and wish we'd found a way of setting up one tertiary college as a pilot.

Bill and Sheila on their wedding day

Despite some differences in approach like this, we always had a good personal relationship. I often went to his house at Crosspool where he lived with his first wife Joan and their poodle, but she had illness and it was difficult at times. When Joan died, and he married Sheila, I was best man and we went to the Anglers Rest at Bamford, where Sheila brought her family, nieces and nephews. They gave Bill a new life, a new extended family. Sheila was able to get him out of England and off on many trips abroad.

He was a very active person right up to the end, and I got the impression that when Bill asked the doctor whether he should carry on after his heart attack, the doctor had felt it would be worse for him not to carry on. **"**

Portraits of a City Father

The FE Colleges

Sheffield's five further education colleges, originally planned as a series of ten, were all in operation by October 1970. The first, Granville College, opened in May 1961, followed by Richmond in 1966, Shirecliffe in 1967 and Stannington in 1970. Stocksbridge College was "imported" after boundary changes.

Eric Wardle played an early role in the development of three of the five. He worked at Granville from 1962 to 1969, most of the time as vice-principal under its first principal George Croft. He was the first principal of Stannington College from 1970 to 1986, part of the team that set it up on a green field site, and from 1986 to 1992 he was principal designate and then principal of Norton College, which he helped establish in an almost derelict building.

His first post at Granville was as lecturer in charge of English and general studies, but soon after his arrival the college was reshaped into departments and he became head of general studies. Howard Smith was appointed vice-principal, and when he moved to Richmond College as its first principal in 1966, Eric Wardle replaced him.

Eric Wardle

"Granville was intended for low level engineering and business studies, with some lower level general education below O level included. People like police cadets and post office telephonists were involved on the general education side. In engineering we were packed to the doors with young apprentices, and it was the same on the business studies side. Less than ten per cent of the students were full-time. All the rest were day release, attending perhaps one day and two nights, or one day and one night. The first principal, George Croft, was in many respects the founding father of the FE colleges.

In those days Granville resembled a large comprehensive school, nothing like the colleges I had known. I moved there from Chesterfield Technical college, which everybody regarded as a 'proper college'. People thought I had taken a step down by moving, but as it turned out that was not to be the case.

There was a steady expansion both in the age range and the range of work - art and design, food and fashion, and health and welfare were installed in the new purpose built block on the south side of Granville Road. The Polytechnic was taking shape and to get room to introduce higher level work at the top they had to push out what they regarded as low level work. To us it was very high level work.

When plans to build Stannington were given the go-ahead in 1968 after some hesitancy, it was planned as an engineering college with a substantial amount of business and secretarial studies - the engineering was intended to fill in the gaps of the provision either at the Polytechnic or at Granville.

The political motivator for all this was Bill Owen, of course. As a lecturer at Granville, I had very little to do with him, but as vice-principal we talked frequently. George Croft, Bill and I frequently talked over possible future development of further education in the city. Bill was very much involved in developments at Granville and was involved in every major event - annual dinners, governors' meetings, which he chaired, open days and open nights - he never missed anything. All you had to do was let him know and he would be there, and the first Mrs Owen was always very supportive as well.

He didn't impress you to look at when you first met him. It was his quiet way of listening to what was being said, taking it all in and then making his statement that impressed you. He never rushed anything.

I shall never forget the way Bill opened up our first open evening. He stood up and he thanked the parents and employers for coming, and generally congratulated the prize winners. Then he went on to say in his slow, deliberate way 'I would like to bet that there is no one in this room tonight who has spent more time in prison than our chief guest.' The chief guest was Fred Mulley MP, of course, and Bill went on to explain that he had spent a long time in prisoner of war camp in Germany. It was an absolute show stopper.

In later years I discovered that Bill Owen had backed me for the principal's post at Stannington, mainly because of what he knew of me from Granville. Stannington was in danger of standing idle because there was no money to provide essential services. Specific accommodation and expensive equipment for welding and fabrication had been built into the college, and the proposal was to leave all this until we had the money to pay caretakers.

Now, many of the staff at Granville were working in holes and corners all over the place, awful places. Fabrication and welding, for instance, was divided partly between the tiers, those workshops that run alongside Pond Street, and partly in an old school in the East End of the city. This traipsing in and out the city for students was very disruptive and bad for discipline because students used to disappear to the pubs or into the pictures. By the time you got up to the workshops there'd only be half of them there.

I was very active in what was then the ATTI and led a deputation to the chief education officer, Michael Harrison, which strongly urged him to open Stannington, saying 'We can't go on like this any longer.' The result was that, ironically, it was the only educational building I know that was finished before time - by September 1969. We simply removed half the engineering from Granville, staff, students, everything, and started business in 1970.

Bill was chair of the governors for the first few years, and I always found him very supportive. He was the kind of chap who expected at least a regular verbal report on what was going on. He expected you to tell him well in advance if there was trouble brewing. But apart from that he left you alone to get on with the job. He never interfered with anything I did, but I know he was quite capable of questioning people and intervening very strongly if he felt things were going wrong. I remember on one occasion he was adjudicating on a matter that had arisen between Stannington College and Shirecliffe College, and frankly I had expected him to go on ad nauseam, but he didn't. He was extremely well briefed and when we got into the room he listened to both sides and immediately said 'Right, there's the decision.' There was no shilly-shallying or anything. It came out like a bullet, that's it.

He hadn't a very obvious sense of humour and was not the kind who told jokes. He would say to us when we were complaining about having no money, 'Aye, they're building a new library in Poly you know, it's going to cost £6-7 millions.' He wasn't slagging off the Polytechnic, he was just teasing us - and he was very good at it. I remember him delaying a meeting for a considerable time - I had the feeling that there was more politics behind it than was apparent because he'd had a difference of opinion with the chairman - while the clerks ran all over the building to check his view that the meeting was not properly constituted unless a woman was present. I think he was being a bit mischievous.

He was very supportive of the tertiary system, although he was worried that the existing FE colleges were going to be interfered with in a way that would prevent them from doing their jobs. For example it was proposed to divide the art and design department at Granville and transfer it to two other colleges. Now he was very jealous of Granville's art and design reputation, which was national and international, and he couldn't see that dividing it was going to improve it.

The official reason was that we ought to have art and design on both the northern and southern sides of the city and I don't think anybody really dissented from that, so most went to Norton and some went to Parkwood. But Bill opposed it for some considerable time. In the same way it was proposed to divide catering, leaving some at Granville and moving the rest to Parson Cross, but there wasn't enough money to do that. The cost of re-equipping kitchens would have been enormous. I think in his heart of hearts Bill saw this as a dismembering - for whatever good reasons - of the system that he had grown up with and nurtured.

When I moved to Norton I saw less of him, of course, but if I met him somewhere and said 'Hello Bill, how are you getting on?' he'd say 'They tell me Norton's not doing so bad.' He obviously kept up to date. **"**

Jack Hall was principal of Shirecliffe College from 1972 until his early retirement in 1989. He first came to Sheffield as one of the few students on the first HND three-year course in the College of Commerce and Technology. Among his fellow students was Irvine Patnick, later MP for Sheffield Hallam. After national service, Jack Hall studied at a teacher training college, worked for five years in Walsall and Wolverhampton and then returned as a tutor at a technical teacher training college.

Jack Hall

" Bill Owen was chairman of Shirecliffe throughout my 17 years. When I took over the college there were 2000 students and 60 staff, and towards the end we had 6000 students and 168 staff. Expansion in areas such as sports, leisure studies, theatre arts and social care - all reflected some aspect of the city's life. There were new developments like full-time courses for 16-18 year olds preparing for a career in social health and welfare. We had the first two-year diploma course in theatre and drama, we developed what was to become a general access course for mature people to higher education and a management centre associated with computer and information technology. Bill brought great stability to Shirecliffe and the other colleges where he was chairman during that period.

With the demise of the steel industry from 1979, the demand for retraining and reskilling dominated our service in the city for some nine years, and this was coordinated through the vice principal Bill Jordan for six years, before his early retirement. We co-ordinated all the retraining that was available in the city, assisting with the problem of redundancy of over 40,000 steelworkers. Bill Owen was very influential and was able to cut through much of the bureaucracy. He was anxious to try and maintain some stability because in the 1920s and 30s he had experienced some of the symptoms of social problems that faced us again. He was a man who had the courage and optimism to pursue a policy even when he was in a minority - he judged issues and people by gut reactions and he was willing to stand by his reactions.

He was different to what I had been used to in previous jobs. He had won the respect of officers and of the opposition in the council chamber. He had the skill to let you know what he wanted if you were sensitive enough and he didn't need to state the bottom line. He was both a persuasive and tolerant man.

Right at the beginning he told me 'Young man, we have policies and I want you to know what they are, and I want to come to you any time I like, and I want you to record your actions for my benefit.' But he didn't try to dictate to me. He was a man of few words in conversation but he absorbed everything and was a listener. He could always make his ideas felt. He was capable in one sentence of saying what some verbose, highly academic, wordsmith would put together in 23 sentences. Behind the scenes he oiled the wheels and made decisions that would have far-reaching consequences for developments in education. That takes a lot of courage and I admire that even today.

I remember being with Bill every year at the annual conference of the Association of Further and Higher Education, where the politicians, the chairman of governors, the director of education or his representative and college principals who were members of the association got together. Those were the times when everybody who had any influence on higher and further education could talk, and out of it emerged new policies.

He had a fund of knowledge - he was what we would call street wise, worldly wise - and he used that in his years on the city council. He drew on it as other intellectuals drew on their knowledge, but he also had an ability to measure actions against social consequences and social needs. He was one of the last politicians in this city who had his heart and his head in socialism whatever he did. He had a fundamental belief 'Do unto others as you would be done by' and he followed that to the letter. He was humble but he wouldn't let people get away with trite comments and patronising behaviour.

There were times when our priorities might have differed. I felt that, like all of us, his political conviction was sometimes tempered by the financial situation and priorities in other sectors of the work of the city. He had always had a great interest in education, possibly at the expense of other services, so there would be resentment in the Labour Group, perhaps from the works department or recreation or libraries. But he had far greater vision than many politicians because of what he had absorbed in his younger days. People respected his ideas.

Education did get his support, and I think he always argued hard to ensure that further education policies were considered as a priority. He believed that educating people would give them a better quality of life, and I think he must have found it galling that he was not always able to articulate that belief. One of the things that must have upset him was that in recent times accountability is on an annual basis, and that cannot stand up because there's a natural cycle in education. Three to five years is needed to prove new courses whether undergraduate, post graduate or diploma.

What worries many of us now when we look back at all the developments that he was involved with over a quarter of a century in higher education is the change to central funding which has made each college principal like a managing director with a balance sheet. Bill argued that you had to have convictions and they start where the need is and the need is your local community.

I've seen him in action in his local community. I remember giving him a lift from the college on one occasion when he had to go to the allotments at Walkley. There was some quite important meeting which he said would only be ten minutes. An hour and a quarter later he emerged. I was never rude to him, but I was livid! He was sorry, but that was the end of it. That was his commitment - straight from a meeting at the college and down to those allotments.

Everybody knew Bill. We had visits at the college from people like Vic

Feather because Bill asked them. When he got on the bus outside the Cathedral they all recognised him, and the driver said 'Move down for t'Lord Mayor!' That was the love and affection people felt for him. **99**

CHAPTER ELEVEN
A Centre of Excellence

Sheffield Polytechnic was created on January 1 1969, the product of a merger between the College of Technology and the College of Art. One of the first three designated polytechnics in the country - 27 more were to follow - its first chairman of governors was Sir Eric Mensforth, its first deputy chairman Bill Owen, then an alderman on Sheffield City Council. When Sir Eric retired in 1975, Bill Owen took over and remained as chairman until 1989 when he again assumed the deputy's role under Peter Newman. Among the governors were many of Sheffield's leading politicians, businessmen, industrialists, educationists and trade unionists.

When he wrote his history of the Polytechnic to celebrate its 21st anniversary in 1990, secretary and clerk to the governing body Tony Davis pinpointed the main reasons why Sheffield College of Technology - "just an area college" - had been included in the first batch of three polytechnics alongside two higher status regional colleges in Hatfield and Sunderland. A crucial factor, he believed, was the strong commitment of Sheffield City Council, not just up to and during the designation process, but right through the Polytechnic's development over the following 20 years.

Among the key people involved, said Tony Davis, were Alderman Albert Ballard, chairman of the council's education committee from 1964 to 1967, his successor Peter Horton, Alderman Harold Slack, chairman of the further education committee until 1965, and his eventual successor, Bill Owen. Two other important figures were chief education officer Michael Harrison and the education officer responsible for further education, Brian Hanson.

The Polytechnic's first principal was the Rev Dr George Tolley, who had

Bill Owen and Tony Davis receiving awards at the City Polytechnic in March 1989, Bill when he finished his Chairmanship of the Board of Governors, and Tony Davis for 21 years as Clerk and Secretary to the Board of Governors.

been senior director of studies at the Royal Air Force College, Cranwell, principal of Worcester Technical College, and head of the chemistry department at Birmingham College of Advanced Technology, now Aston University.

He had come to Sheffield in September 1966 as principal of the College of Technology, guided it through its transformation to polytechnic and stayed on as principal until early retirement in December 1982. By the time he handed over to his successor, John Stoddart, the Polytechnic's roster of full-time and sandwich students had grown from about 1,650 to 7,600, there were more than 4,500 part-time students and his 160 full time teaching staff had become 800.

The Polytechnic had become a force within the city, important nationally as well as locally, attracting full-time students from all over the country, many of whom stayed on to live and work in Sheffield. The impact on the city itself was considerable, both economically through salaries bills and supplies, and in the sheer scale of educational training provided. Relationships were strengthened with businesses and professional services, with estate agents and surveyors.

Bill (second from right) with George Tolley; Edward Simpson, Deputy Secretary of the DES and Sir Eric Mensforth, Chairman of the Board of Governors of Sheffield Polytechnic in 1975.

George Tolley

"Certainly I saw very strong development of allegiances and pride in industry and business, especially in their attitude towards the Polytechnic - because it's fair to say that when I came here in 1966 the College of Technology was a rather big night school and it was looked upon as such.

The general view was that the Tech was a place where you went for part-time courses while other work was going on. That changed very rapidly and it came to be regarded as a national centre of higher education, a centre of excellence in engineering and metallurgy, business studies, estate management and so on.

Bill Owen was the backroom operator through this period. He was a member of the committee which appointed me principal of the College of Technology, and he was on the governing body throughout the course of the whole period that I was at the Polytechnic. He was either deputy chairman or chairman, so I was always closely associated with him.

Frankly he was never a very good front of stage man. We knew it, and he knew it. But he was the link with the Labour Group and no decision of any significance was ever taken about local authority expenditure without Labour Group approval. Even though we had our own board of governors, important policy decisions still had to be cleared through the city council - and that meant through the Labour Group.

Bill was always very good at making contacts, smoothing the path, lobbying where lobbying was necessary - and it often was, because he had some awkward colleagues. For quite a long time it was clear that there was no great commitment at city council to the Polytechnic. I think they regarded it as - well not quite as a cuckoo in the nest, but as an organisation that was perhaps grown too big for its own boots.

Many city councillors felt that the colleges of further education were all right because they were strictly local, they were relatively small and controllable. On the other hand the Polytechnic was getting out of hand and it was national and we were attracting all these full-time students from all over the country.

There was a selling job to be done and a great deal of that was public selling, both to the city council and to business. But there were also many quiet discussions in corridors, and in backrooms. Bill spent a lot of time on persuasion - and he was good at it, because he was respected. If Bill Owen said it was all right, it was all right.

Bill also was very effective in carrying the trade union movement in the city with the Polytechnic. We needed their support because of their direct links with the city council. We needed it also for the widening range of course provisions which really were changing the nature of training in significant ways.

Bill was operating as president of the trades and labour council so it was all done very quietly and for the most part effectively. We had our battles and some we lost, some we won. Most of the really big battles we had with the city council were not public, of course. They were sometimes over the scale of development - should we be expanding to 5,000 students, or should we settle for 2,500 students.

There were also battles over expenditure. Although none of the Polytechnic's spending on higher education was ever a direct charge on the rates, many city councillors tried to present some of these issues as a charge on the rates. Capital was a different problem. There was always a feeling around that the Polytechnic's capital requirements were denying other capital development schemes. So there were a lot of discussions about new building developments and, by and large, we did not do very well in my years.

There were battles also that had to be fought about changes in conditions of service. Whatever we did clearly had implications for the rest of the city council's services and we were going very strongly down the line of multi-skilling and flexible working.

Just before I left the Polytechnic we were investing in a new computer installation to replace the old one, and we had prepared very carefully for a detailed specification. We had decided that it had to be an IBM computer although there were strong ideas amongst city councillors that you should buy British, ICL. The city council had bought ICL but the Japanese content of an ICL computer was 75 percent compared with 25 percent of an IBM computer.

There was a great battle which went on for about six or seven months when we flitted in and out of the leader of the city council David Blunkett's office. We were trying to hold a line that whatever we bought had to be effective in its use.

Bill didn't always take my point, I wouldn't have expected him to, but his line in these things was to press very hard, saying 'Look, we have a competent staff at the Polytechnic, we have a competent principal. They do their job well, they do their job carefully, and you city councillors, whether you're the leader' and he'd wag his finger at old George Wilson and David Blunkett, 'have got to listen. You've got to listen to George!'

Bill was always adept at introducing a practical tone to the discussion to get away from political posturing. 'This is the decision that's got to be taken, never mind the frills ... and you've got to listen to what the Polytechnic is saying, otherwise you'll make a fool of yourself.' And that was the line that came through.

He had this tremendous gift of mastering the brief. He would never have called it that, but that is what it was. He had a tremendous skill in doing his homework, reading his papers very carefully, asking very few questions - but what questions there were cut through to the heart of the matter. He never had to fumble through his papers in a meeting, he knew what was going on, the essential issues.

My job was to be the front man and I accepted it as such. There were times when I felt that things really had to be put very firmly on the line in the public domain, even if that meant upsetting city councillors, or upsetting leaders nationally, and Bill accepted that even though it sometimes made life very difficult for him.

His colleagues would ask 'What's George Tolley going on about again, and why is he criticising the city council when we've done all this for the Polytechnic?' But never once - even though on some occasions I was pretty hard hitting with the city council - never once did Bill ever say to me 'You've to pull back.' His line was 'If you've thought about it carefully and that's your decision, I'll back you.'

I remember an argument over expenditure and it was put over in the press as a personal slanging match between myself and Peter Horton, the chairman of the education committee. That was painful for Bill because he was deputy chairman of the education committee at the time. He wanted to be totally loyal to the education committee and to the governors. He could easily have pulled the plug but he didn't. Peter Horton and I sat down with Bill and David Blunkett and agreed a formula whereby we could at any rate agree in public. It also resulted in certain adjustments being made to the Polytechnic budget.

Through all of this Bill didn't say very much to me because he never did say very much. Everyone will say the same about Bill, that he was a very quiet, very reticent man, but he didn't have to say very much. You knew what he was thinking. You also knew that he was very straight. If Bill said one thing to me I knew he was saying the same thing to the Labour Group. Bill was not in the business of carrying bits and pieces of information from one side to the other. He was an advocate on behalf of the Polytechnic in places where it mattered.

I never found any reason to question his belief in the Polytechnic and its role in education, though I would have to say that in my view Bill's heart was much more with Granville than it was with the Polytechnic. I'm not trying to belittle anything that he did with the Polytechnic, but I would say his heart was really with Granville, because he felt a much greater affinity with the level of work that was going on there.

But he was committed to the Polytechnic and was utterly convinced that what we were trying to achieve in building up a nationally recognised centre of higher education was absolutely right for the city. He understood that. He certainly never stinted on his time with us. We had our briefing meetings prior to governing body meetings and Bill would come to the many social occasions when we were entertaining people from outside.

I had a very good relationship with him. He was not demonstrative and in some ways he could be offputting. I've talked before about 'Bill's formidable silences' - and they were formidable. There have been many occasions when we've had a dinner at the Polytechnic, maybe a dozen round the table, and I mean important, significant people. Most of them have opened up and talked about all sorts of issues but Bill has sat there and not said a word, not a word. There are many people who would be upset by that, who would think that he wasn't interested. But he would be taking everything in. Knowing Bill really well, the silences never worried me but I know they worried other people.

We had a very good understanding, maybe for three reasons. One was that I'm a Black Countryman and Bill's parents were from the Black Country and origins matter a lot with Bill. The second reason I think was that I'm from a working class background and I grew up during the unemployment years when my father was out of work for three years. That background was something Bill could immediately relate to. The third reason was personal and it occurred when Bill's first wife Joan died. That brought us closer together. I counselled Bill about some of the aspects of bereavement and talked to him in a personal way.

It didn't make him any more demonstrative. It didn't make him more talkative. But we always had a very good personal understanding and it was very rare for us to have any meeting at all without having a few jokes between us - very quietly. He had a wry sense of humour, very witty, just the odd phrase dropped into a conversation, often enough when he wasn't participating and you thought he was miles away, when he looked miles away.

We seldom talked about politics. We would discuss political events and we'd discuss political personalities as everybody does but it was principles with Bill really. He wasn't interested in your politics. I was never conscious of him storing up anything about the political opinions of a member of the staff at the Polytechnic.

I always felt, and indeed I always was, absolutely open with him. If I wanted to say something very blunt and perhaps not very complimentary about the city council I would say it to him and he would take it, and there was never any question of saying 'We mustn't talk like that about the city council.'

Bill Owen was a very highly educated man of course, not in a formal sense but in terms of knowledge and appreciation and understanding of books and art. He had a remarkable breadth and depth of knowledge. I remember one of those dinners I mentioned, with quite an illustrious table, and Bill was his usual silent self, not registering with anybody at all until about half way through the main course when somebody across the table mentioned visiting the Turner exhibition at the Tate. Somebody else picked this up, and Bill suddenly said ' I like Turner' and launched into a twenty minute exposition of Turner's paintings which had everybody hanging on his words. It was brilliant! I mean this was an art critic who'd suddenly taken over, and I had no idea that he'd any interest in Turner at all. He ran through a number of paintings and the quality of what he was saying was really quite brilliant. And then having said it, he shut up - that was it!

After I left the Polytechnic we'd meet at a number of Polytechnic social occasions and on other city occasions and we'd have a chat. He was always interested in catching up with what I was doing, as I was with him. We never lost that ease of relationship.

His greatest contribution was that he was a great supporter. Bill wasn't a person who breezed into a place and said 'Look, we've got to do this.' That wasn't his style. His style was saying 'Right, what do we need to do?' And when that had been decided 'I will back you.' That was tremendously important, particularly in a political place like Sheffield. 🙶

C H A P T E R   T W E L V E

Polytechnic to University

John Stoddart succeeded George Tolley as principal of Sheffield Polytechnic in 1983, moving from Hull where he had been director of Humberside College of Higher Education from 1976. He already knew something of the Polytechnic - from 1970 to 1972 he had been its head of economics and business studies.

In the ten years after his appointment, the Polytechnic continued to grow, and he steered it through its transition into Sheffield Hallam University in 1992. It now has about 20,000 students, with teaching staff relatively stable between 750 and 860, an impressive rise in "productivity." Local involvement has increased through support for small companies, community groups, and the city council's range of activities. A balance has been maintained between diploma, degree, postgraduate, and part-time work, and student choice and flexibility has been increased.

The University's fabric, too, has been improved over the last decade. Its libraries have expanded, the Sheffield Science Park was developed in partnership with English Estates, the University of Sheffield and the local authority. The recent £27 million building project due to be completed by the end of 1993 will provide two new engineering blocks and an administration block.

John Stoddart

❝ When I was at the Polytechnic in the '70s I knew Bill Owen only as a vague figure and of course by reputation. I got to know him well after he chaired the interview board in 1983. Even the offer of appointment was very much typical of Bill. I answered the phone and he said 'This is Owen, Sheffield. Our chief education officer will be in touch with yours to arrange when you start!' And I said 'Does that mean you are offering me the job - because if it does there are various things we should talk about.'

I soon found that Bill's style was to use the professionals and to listen to the professionals. That wasn't to say that he didn't have his own views and didn't make them known. If he disagreed with the professionals he would say so, but he listened and he didn't interfere except on matters of principle. It was very rare that he got off principle and into detail.

He seemed to me very clear about what he perceived his role as chair of governors to be, and what he perceived his role as an elder statesman to be - someone to whom you could turn for advice. He would say 'If you do that it will cause the following reactions,' which was a nice way of saying 'Well, I wouldn't if I were you, but it's your decision.'

Herol 'Bomber' Graham receiving his Honorary Fellowship scroll from Bill in 1990 watched by Chaplain Leslie Green and John Stoddart, Principal of the Polytechnic.

He wanted to make sure the Polytechnic remained an asset for the area and true to its mission, to control the broad mission and character of the institution, and particularly in his final years, to be able to counsel and advise. Since it became a university, and perhaps a little before that, he was aware that others had a strong contribution to make, so he always sat there bringing things together rather than attempting to steer the Board. It was a very special skill.

In a way Bill 'owned' the Polytechnic and he developed with it, but for somebody who'd been involved for more than 20 years to be able to sit back and steer rather than get involved in detail is a marvellous achievement. And I'm sure that was the key at the end, that Bill felt it was very much his creation, something he'd fight for.

Once I got to know him I found him tremendous. I found his sense of humour amazing. He had an ability to wind up people and to bring home to them that they were being pompous - he'd have a way of letting you go on before he said 'Do you mean ...?' And in the last year or two, when his hearing was going, he had a habit of waiting until the very last minute before intervening, and you were never sure whether it was his hearing or whether it was Bill just being Bill. He'd quite often come back to an agenda item after you'd left it, or thought you'd left it.

I think it was at the party to celebrate 21 years of the Polytechnic that Leslie Green who had been chaplain for about 23 years and had worked with Bill, delivered a broadside on how things had changed - and not always for the better. How higher education had changed, how education had changed, how the Polytechnic had changed, how he remembered a time when you had time to take care of students. This went on for ten or fifteen minutes and at the end Bill stood up and said 'Thank you, Reverend Green. Now we know why they blocked your door up!' He brought the place down, because we had just moved Leslie to an office downstairs, blocked up the door of his old office and converted it into a bigger room. Leslie had obviously been complaining about it to Bill.

There was another instance when we were interviewing for head of design and Bill took a sketch out of his pocket, passed it across and said 'What do you think of that?' It was a dove of peace that Picasso had drawn for Bill when he visited the city. The applicants were quite startled by this. I think he'd talk about art rather more than he'd talk about adult education. He'd always talk about politics, of course. He'd always return to a golden era which appeared to be around the Wilson era which must have been the heyday of Bill's power. He'd relate back in education to Shirley Williams and not so much to Crosland. He'd talk about Shirley Williams, talk about Ted Short, they seemed to be the national education politicians with whom he identified.

He needed convincing about the Polytechnic becoming a university, as we all did, but he was more concerned with the realities than the trappings, more concerned with what it would mean in terms of governors, more concerned about accountability and links with the local authority, and whether we would engage in educational academic drift. I think he saw very clearly that it would be to the students' advantage, and once the local authority's formal connection had gone, he saw the logic of binary going, although he was also worried about the image we would have with the Town Hall. But I think at the end he felt he couldn't affect that. He felt marginalised from the Labour group, although he was an incredibly loyal attender and a fighter even if he didn't believe in particular decisions.

The great thing about Bill was trust. He was trusted and he had all sorts of links with what were, in my terms, 'vested interest' groups. I certainly had confidence in Bill to make his own judgements no matter what was said to him. So I knew if he was listening to the unions he would probably give as good as he got. He would explain my point of view to them.

His greatest contribution from my point of view was wise counsel. He might have had great ambitions and great visions for the institution but he didn't articulate them. What he did do was to listen and enable, to help and to steer, and to allow other people to achieve. I think he should have retired from the vice chairmanship and maybe the chairmanship a little earlier, but I don't think he should have retired as a governor. That's not because I think we owed him anything, but because he provided the background and experience which would have been impossible to duplicate. He was as bright as a button anyway. And he still came to meetings with all his papers marked. He had read them, and he knew which items he was going to speak on.

He was a very close friend, not in everyday life perhaps, but I always felt that if there was a particular problem I could have gone to Bill. I didn't normally do that, but nevertheless he was there, and you felt that you could if you wanted to.

He and Sheila were both unstinting with their time. If you asked them to do anything they would do it. And they didn't intrude, they didn't push themselves. They didn't come along saying 'Can I do this, will I do this?' We have a number of visits every year of officials or people prominent in national and local positions. Bill would always come if he was invited and if he wasn't invited, and somebody else did it, he was always happy about it. **" "**

The Polytechnic's administration chief for 20 years, Tony Davis was appointed as secretary and clerk to the governing body in 1969 after working for nearly 15 years in Nyasaland/Malawi, from 1955 until 1964 in the Overseas Civil Service. When Malawi became independent he was seconded to the Malawi government until 1968, becoming chief education officer. He retired from the Polytechnic in March 1989, three years before it became a university.

Tony Davis **"** I came to work in Sheffield in the one year in the last 50 when the Conservatives were in power, and Frank Adams was chairman of the governors. He was someone for whom Bill had a lot of time. In fact Bill had a high regard for anyone who made contributions to the city, irrespective of their political colour.

I was a bit bewildered and bemused in my first months here because the polytechnics were new, especially to somebody who had been away from England for 15 years, and George Tolley took a bit of a gamble with me. It was a tough number, and George Tolley was a tough boss. In the 25 years since then we've become close friends, but I had my problems and Bill was a very helpful intermediary. I'm always grateful to Bill for that.

I know his public speaking was not his strong point, but it's a great pity that many thousands of people only saw Bill on the stage at the conferment ceremony in the City Hall. What he said was genuine and down to earth. He was obviously a Sheffielder welcoming visitors from outside, very much part of the city. For a man whose education had been limited - in terms of years, not in terms of what he'd learned - he had a care and concern for education that was typical of his time. This was reflected in the range of governing bodies of which he was chairman. I don't know how he managed to juggle it all at the same time.

He was extremely shrewd in meetings. You could never get round him. Even George Caborn found Bill a pretty shrewd operator as chairman when he wanted to bulldoze anything through or short-cut anything. And he was an under-rated organiser of a meeting. He was always willing to pick up advice from the secretary next to him without being obvious. Some chairmen will say 'Oh right, I've heard what you said, thank you very much' but Bill would just pick it up quietly and use it. Sometimes you'd prepare a little speech for him to say at the conferment ceremony, for example, and you'd find him reading it word for word. The next year you could hardly recognise it. I think he was more agile in his use of English than people realised when they just heard him do a set piece in a public place.

His great strengths were his honesty, integrity, and his interest and support for those working in the institution. He was totally supportive of the Poly and fought our corner very hard in the early years when the local authority had quite a strong influence. Those were the days when if you wanted a clerical officer for the Polytechnic you had to go through the council's committee structure. Bill spent his whole life weighing people up, employers or his fellow employees.

Sometimes in a meeting he would pick up something you'd said and perhaps go a bit too far with it. One or two of our staff who were members of the governing body by election were rubbed a bit the wrong way at times, because he had some difficulty in accepting our general withdrawal from local authority control. A lot of people had that problem. I remember George Tolley asking me one day about a very close friend of mine who'd just come over from the local authority 'Do you think we can trust him?' George didn't mean that in any underhand way. He was really asking 'Is he a Polytechnic man?'

Nationally we were being drawn out of local authority control and in a sense we were testing our wings. We went through a bad stage in the middle '70s when the local authority were asking questions like 'Why aren't you using our abattoir for your meat?' The reason was that it took about two days for a special delivery whereas Joe Smith round the corner could produce the same item in half an hour. 'And why don't you use our printing department?' Well, we had a budget and we could get it cheaper elsewhere, and that was supposed to be their criterion anyway.

Bill would sometimes tell us 'You can't do that' - not because it was illegal, but because it went against policy, or because it was best left until he had had a word with someone. I think he had some difficulty about things like the central meat department and the printing department. And I don't think we always appreciated that he'd be under fire from colleagues who would say 'You're our man in the Poly, why are you allowing that?'

But Bill and Peter Horton were committed, and everybody realised that. People realised also they could depend on them, they found time and they kept their word, and they got respect from 'the other side'.

Bill always had time. He might be late occasionally, but he always seemed to have time.

His second wife Sheila was a great influence on him in a very good way - he almost changed overnight in a sense. I didn't know Joan very well, but she was very much the traditional waiting at home for Bill person, no less strong and helpful in that respect. But Sheila was different and brought him out a bit, and we were all pleased to see that. My wife and I looked on Bill as a friend and we knew we could talk to him about anything. Bill had a puckish sense of humour and whenever I drove him to and from college he would show it in wonderful anecdotes about his life and colleagues in local government and the unions. **"**

Bill Owen stepped down as chairman of the board of governors in 1989 but continued as deputy chairman until his death. His 22 year long involvement with the institution in one role or another had bracketed its growth from College of Technology to University, and both Polytechnic and University have continued to show gratitude. Bill Owen was made an Honorary Fellow in 1976. A specially commissioned portrait hangs in the offices of the principal, close to another of Dr George Tolley, its first head.

The new chairman of the governors, Peter Newman, came to the Polytechnic from a very different background. An engineer who read mechanical sciences at Cambridge, he joined Davy United Engineering Company in 1960 and after a graduate apprenticeship became a junior development engineer, moved into commercial administration, and after nine years with a subsidiary based in Dorset, returned to Sheffield as Managing Director of Davy McKee in 1984.

He became a director of Sheffield Development Corporation and later a member of the Cutlers' Company. In 1987 he was promoted to run the Davy Metals Division of Companies scattered throughout the UK, France, United States, Canada, Chile and South Africa, and then to the main board in London. When Davy was bought by Trafalgar House at the end of 1991, he left the company.

Peter Newman

"When I came back to Sheffield in 1984 it was a scarred city and Davy seemed to want no part of it - both had suffered from the problems in the steel industry and from the open warfare between town and business. I felt we needed to overcome that, and when Michael Jarratt, vicar of Ranmoor Church, ran a series of forums or seminars which attempted to bring together the warring parties under an ecumenical church wing, I became involved.

About that time I met John Stoddart and I was invited to become a governor of the Polytechnic with Bill Owen as my chairman. That was the first time I'd met him because I hadn't been in Sheffield over the previous ten years and perhaps that helped. There was so much bitterness around, real bitterness, on both sides, but Bill never showed it to me and I was oblivious to it from other sources because I hadn't been part of it. We approached each other as new people, with no hang-ups, and no background.

There could have been problems with the board at that time because it was almost unhandleable by my standards. Bill handled it because he came from a different background. My experience was of very tight boards of people who tended to think the same way, and I had no experience of the diversity and the size of that board. There were about three dozen members and with backers and officers you could easily have 50 people in the room. That was an environment that Bill thrived in. It was the town hall environment, so he was very much at home. But it was very difficult to know what the board thought it was there for, because the Poly belonged to the town hall, and was very well run by the town hall - and educationally it was damn good.

In the lead-up to incorporation, I was asked to chair the formation committee, whose main task was to form the new board. The committee became the formation board which ran in parallel with Bill's board very amicably. There were no problems and through Bill's membership of both groups we kept each other informed. Bill worked very smoothly with me and, of course, eventually handed over on incorporation day, April 1 1989.

When he was in the chair, Bill would exert authority in any debate that got out of hand quite ruthlessly and very professionally. He was an old pro, no question about that, and he could handle people, angry people who had lost their cool. It's an arena that mercifully I haven't had to deal with, because with incorporation came the smaller board and independence.

Independence was two-sided of course. It was a threat and an opportunity. The threat was that all the things we took for granted could be taken away, mundane things like payroll, which was done by the town hall, like financial control and half the governors - all suddenly cut off. Had that been done badly, with a sense of pique, it would have been disastrous for the institution.

The opportunities grew out of being a fully fledged educational establishment in its own right, with its own personality, free to flex its wings. It had grown up, it was 21 years old in 1990, and there was a feeling that polytechnics had literally come of age and should be listened to in their own right.

If you think of the explosive mixture of a town hall that was sensitised against people like me - industrialists - having to hand over the people's assets, buildings, millions of pounds worth of buildings which were part of the fabric of the city of Sheffield, the fact that it was done so extraordinarily smoothly has to be part of the gift of Bill Owen. Bill must have been pivotal in ensuring it was done smoothly, and I imagine he must have said 'Well, Newman's all right.' There's no way I would have got that job if he hadn't said that, because Bill's opinion was very much sought.

The next phase in our relationship was when Bill became my deputy chairman. He handled it with the utmost of ease, not the slightest hiccup of any resentment or even bad temper. I took it for granted at the time, but looking back on it now, I think it was quite remarkable. I don't think I've done as well when I've handed over jobs to younger people. He was rumbustious, of course. I think he felt slightly freer being a deputy chairman or normal board member, and he was much more involved in debates than he had been as chairman.

I certainly never felt threatened or undermined. He had his arguments up front - and he could be very argumentative. He was quite ruthless in winning his way, right or wrong, although that's subjective. But if he thought something was right, he'd go hell for leather to achieve it. He would make certain he got the politics right and chatted up the right people before meetings. His techniques were amusing and some of them I think were mischievous - playing on his deafness to some extent, and when we were on agenda item 15 he'd suddenly start talking about agenda item 5 as if you'd never left it. It was wonderful timing because it really got everyone's attention. People suddenly started thinking silly old man, he really is a bit confused.

But no way was he confused. He was making a dramatic entrance again to make his point.

I thought he was right to stay on as deputy chairman, with the only caveat his own health. He was frail towards the end, but the old sparkle was there on occasions. Right up to his last meeting he was making points and guiding me. It's a lonely job being a chairman, not an awful lot of people to talk to. I've learned now to talk with my fellow chairmen around the country, but in the early days the only person I had to talk to was Bill. Obviously I'd talk to John Stoddart about general issues, but I couldn't talk about the things that were very subjective to the principal. The only person a chairman can talk with openly is his deputy chairman, and Bill was a very ready listener. **"**

Portraits of a City Father

CHAPTER THIRTEEN

Ruskin of the North

Access to education was a motivating force throughout Bill Owen's life. As a young man he had sought it for himself through the Workers Educational Association and other similar organisations. Decades later, as a city councillor, he encouraged its provision through youth training, further and adult education colleges. By the time "access" had become a fashionable educational concept of the 1970s, and before the Russell Report on adult education gave the green light for more adult residential education, Bill Owen and a group of educationists with similar ambitions had already outlined plans for Northern College, their own "Ruskin College of the North".

Northern College opened its doors in 1978, transforming Wentworth Castle near Barnsley from a teachers' training college into a centre of liberal studies for up to 140 working people. Half of them would take two-year residential courses, others would arrive for anything from a few days at weekends to a couple of weeks for courses tailormade to meet their special needs in the community.

The initiative for the college had come from Sheffield, later joined in a consortium of Yorkshire education authorities by Barnsley, Doncaster and Rotherham. Among the working group who studied the idea's feasibility were Bill Owen, Royden Harrison and Michael Barratt Brown, lecturers at the University of Sheffield's extramural department, Roy Bailey, head of Sheffield City Polytechnic's department of applied social studies, and education officer Bill Carter.

Michael Barratt Brown became the college's first principal and remained at its head until his retirement in 1983. He had come to Sheffield in 1959 as lecturer on industrial studies in the extra mural department, working largely with local trade unions, and helping to establish courses for mineworkers who came to the University one or two days a week. These courses were eventually extended to the steel industry, engineering, fire brigades, and local government.

❝ One of the first people I met with Royden Harrison was Bill Owen. Bill typified the trades and labour council where you had a mixture of political views that included not only Labour Party but also Communist and other parties. His capacity to pull people together was the first thing that impressed me, and he did it not by banging people on the head but by listening to them.

Michael Barratt Brown

Quite early on, he used me to write pieces of speeches and ideas for things he would say when he got to Labour Party conferences. He had no problem about what to say in his own bailiwick, but when he wanted a wider audience, Royden Harrison and I used to write things for him. At my first meeting in that office of his, where you had to climb in over the books and clear a space in the paper and files, I quickly discovered that this was not simply a trade union official but an extremely widely read man, who was an intellectual comrade as well as a political trade union comrade.

We worked officially together to extend day release provision for the engineering industry, and we were able to inject a certain amount of liberal studies into what otherwise might have been rather narrow minded. And that was typical of Bill, not only to bring people together, but to want wider educational rather than a narrow vocational provision. We ran a number of courses for full-time officers which Bill attended as a student for a time, and that again was typical - he didn't mind in the least becoming a student, though I don't think he ever wrote an essay. I don't think he had time.

For some years it had been obvious to most of us in the WEA and in the extramural department that we were encouraging people to go on from either one day a week courses or weekend classes to longer education at Ruskin,

Harlech, the Co-op College or Fircroft, but there was no local college to which people could go. I talked about this with Bill and with Bert Winn, who was the leader of the Derbyshire mineworkers, and we even tried to put in a bid for Queen Anne's Crescent at Buxton, which is now in some disrepair. It was up for sale and we thought it would make a splendid college for Derbyshire, but nobody was prepared to put that kind of money up.

When the Russell Committee came to Sheffield, four of us - Bill Carter, Roy Bailey, Ray Fisher the WEA secretary and I - told them we needed a Ruskin of the North, and we got a recommendation in the report that there should be one further long term residential college in the north of England.

I don't think we'd have got it without Bill Owen - in fact, I'm sure we wouldn't. But we wouldn't have got it in any case without the connection between Bill Owen and the new local government authorities which were established in South Yorkshire. The day I discovered that half my students seemed to be councillors on these various authorities was the day it became quite clear that it would be possible to have a college, because there would be such very strong support for it from the councils.

At almost the same time it was announced that a number of teacher training colleges were going to be closed, among them Wentworth Castle. I decided it was absolutely right for us, because it was small and we could have the whole of it. The problem about all the other colleges was we would be a poor relation in a huge college site like Wentworth Woodhouse, the Poly, or Doncaster.

And here was a problem for Bill, because he really wanted that college in Sheffield, no question about it. On the other hand he was extremely realistic and knew he probably wouldn't get it, because the argument for Barnsley was very strong - they didn't have any higher education or further education institution if they lost the teacher training college.

We still had to persuade the Labour government that a residential college was needed, because we wanted scholarships for two year courses. But it was strongly felt that the college should also be for people who came for a weekend or a week so that it would be a part of the local educational provision, with some input of funds from local authorities. Now Ruskin and the other colleges were simply financed from central government, still are largely, so this was a new proposition and would have been completely impossible without the commitment of those four authorities. We managed to get them to fill the gap when central government came back with a derisory sum of money on top of the scholarships for students. It meant that the four authorities would have to put up the cash, so we set up a consortium to establish the college. It would not have happened, however, without constant pressure from Bill Owen and Peter Horton on the other Labour leaders in the four authorities.

I got to know Bill well in those early days because we really had a lot of difficulties. Cuts had already begun to be made, even by a Labour government, and there were teething problems in getting money out of the authorities who had agreed to finance a certain number of students. You don't get in any one year exactly the right number of students from each authority, and Rotherham was beginning to say 'Hey, we don't seem to have a student this year.' Sheffield had excellent adult education provision which could find people who wanted to go on and study, and Sheffield was happy to encourage them to take residential or short courses. Encouraging other authorities was much more difficult, but Bill was a tower of strength in persuading them that their day would come.

The two year course inevitably became a route into university, though we didn't want it to be so. Rising unemployment rates made that happen. We thought a lot of people would go back into the trade union movement or into social work and community care.

We made two big changes from Ruskin. We tried to have equal numbers of women, and we put as much emphasis on short courses and short course students as on the longer courses. To do that, we said there would be no qualification for entry on any of the courses, whereas Ruskin and the other colleges always asked entrants to write a long essay. That meant we built in the idea of moving from say a weekend course to a week, maybe even a two week course, building up to attending the college on a two year course.

We had some drop-outs, but there were very few. We went through a thorough interviewing procedure, and we looked for evidence that people had made some attempt at studying. Usually they had been to a WEA class, an adult education centre, or to a trade union course. When they came in for an interview, they came for a whole night and a whole day. In a sense, the biggest difficulty we faced in the early months was persuading the long course students to accept people who occupied 'their' house and 'their' college just for a week, who made an awful noise and brought the children. We solved that because I had one remarkable president of the students union who simply said 'On Sunday I'm going to have the Students Union welcome the short course students.' The president told them what was expected of them, how the house and buildings were used, and generally made them feel welcome. It was a brilliant idea and there were no problems after that.

It didn't only work administratively, it worked educationally, because all the people on the short course came in to a learning atmosphere, and the people on the long course were constantly kept in touch with the fact that there was a real world out there. That mix has continued and in my view is the greatest success of the whole institution.

Although the long course students have mainly gone on to universities, and though some of the short course student have gone on to study on long courses, by far the greatest number came in to improve their capacity in the voluntary work they were doing or, as unemployment increased, to improve their capacity to do something with their period of unemployment. Mostly they were people wishing to make a bigger contribution to their communities - and they came to us not simply to learn something that we had to teach, they came to study their problem. It might have been how to deal with the local housing officer, how to set up a co-operative, how to get all the different agencies who supported different kinds of illness in a hospital to work together.

The college became a marvellous resource centre where they could get help and support, but it was also a place of peace where they could get away from the day to day struggle and think quietly about their problems. And it needed somebody like Bill Owen to understand that you didn't solely measure success by O levels or A levels or certificates or diplomas - though we were very rigorous about those - but that you should judge the place by the contribution it could make to the community.

We had difficulties finding the catering staff required to run a college with a hundred beds at the beginning, extended later to about 140 or so. We had complaints about food and accommodation, and there were administrative problems in managing the bar and use of the bar, and I found Bill absolutely invaluable in some difficult battles.

One of the things he was marvellous about was that we were anxious to make it a college for women as well as men, and we persuaded the Rowntree Trust to give us some money to convert one of the buildings into a creche. But the real problem was that we wanted to have single parents who had older children. We were able to persuade the local schools to take them but, of course, the children occupied a bed. Now a bed as far as we were concerned was money. But Bill was always concerned to aim at a 50/50 balance and the only way to do that was to accept the fact that while men could come and leave their families behind, often women couldn't.

He was also extremely helpful in expanding the number of authorities we were able to pull in to help to finance the college by sending students - not only Leeds and Humberside which were the obvious ones, but Bradford and others which were not necessarily Labour authorities.

As a person, Bill was a very odd mixture. He was not what you'd call a warm chap. He had a cold handshake, he didn't really look you in the eye very clearly, and yet in a funny sort of way you always felt that he was close to you. I suppose that was because he was such a very good listener, and because when he did say his piece it was absolutely bang on and showed he'd been listening carefully and thinking very hard.

When I retired they gave a splendid party for me. Bill made a speech and said very nice things about how we'd worked together, and I think that really was true. Between us, we can take a lot of the responsibility for there being a Northern College. **99**

Roy Bailey joined the staff of Sheffield Polytechnic in 1971 as head of the new department of Applied Social Studies, responsible for the development of social work, sociology and psychology. He remained head of department for nearly 20 years before retiring to concentrate on an international career as a folk singer. During that time he was Dean of the Faculties of Social Studies and later of Education, Health and Welfare, a member of the Council of Management of the Northern College and its staffing committee, an external examiner and chief examiner.

Two years after arriving in Sheffield, he became chairman of the adult and continuing education committee. When the small group working informally on the idea of a residential northern college of adult education was formed, Roy was asked to join it.

Roy Bailey **66** That's how I met Bill Owen and we became quite firm friends from that moment on. We met formally at meetings. He learned that I was a musician and a singer and he talked about his interest in music, and I think he slowly acquired every record I made. He often talked about music and his background with the Workers Music Association some years before.

While we were working together on developing and establishing the Northern College, I remember looking for a site. We had established a steering committee of the four South Yorkshire authorities, got various approvals and good signs from the Department of Education and Science as it was then, and we had gone on the road, as it were, looking for sites. One was the Lady Mabel College in Rotherham which was subsequently to become part of Sheffield City Polytechnic but at that time was still an independent college.

We were walking through the grounds and he stopped me at one point and put his arm on my shoulder and said 'Roy, we don't wear suede shoes in the north!' I had a pair of suede shoes on, and I thought 'Oh!' I wasn't sure what he was saying but I guessed it was 'only southerners and softies wear suede shoes.' I've never worn suede shoes since.

We had that kind of relationship which was quite informal and friendly as well as formal on committees, and that was to be a characteristic of our relationship throughout the years that I knew him.

He became the first vice-chairman of the council of management of the Northern College and later the chairman, and I was the Poly's representative on that body. We worked together on the staffing committee, and on subcommittees of the council of management. I was always very flattered by the fact that he would listen to what I would say, and he would give me the impression that if he didn't always agree with my position he always listened and valued that position. I was proud that I could think of us as friends.

I remember an appointments committee we were on together at the college and two people, X and Y, applied for quite a senior post. Most of the committee was in favour of appointing Y, and usually I tend to think when you get to a shortlist either of the people can do the job and would grow into it. But in this case I was committed to X. I knew him and believed he was the right person for that job, so I held out. Bill said nothing. There was strong argument and I thought I was in the minority. Suddenly Bill chimed up and said 'I'm going to go with Roy, I value his comments, value his opinion.' Eventually X was appointed and a year or so later the other people on the committee who had been opposed to X wrote me a letter saying I was right. Bill said to me 'I'm glad I went with you, it was right wasn't it?' And I said

'Well I think so, and I think you knew.'

One of his characteristics was that he gave the impression that he wasn't involved in the discussions that were taking place. We'd sit in innumerable committees and discussions would be going on, getting quite fierce at times, and Bill would seem to be totally uninvolved. In fact you wondered if he'd gone to sleep. And then he'd look up and he'd say something which made it quite clear he'd been listening to everything that had gone on, and usually his contribution was extremely succinct and without any of the academic flannel that we all use to qualify our positions. He would simply say 'This is what I think, having listened' and most of us realised that was what we were trying to achieve. He never dragged us or dominated us. He was never a tyrant.

I think he was an unreconstructed socialist, very unfashionable these days. He believed in issues like 'equality' and 'equality of opportunity'. He believed that people were equal and that they deserved equal treatment. They may be more or less skilled, or more or less intellectual, or more or less successful, but he wanted to create circumstances where everybody had an opportunity to achieve their full potential. Those expressions in the 90s sound rather odd, but he was motivated by them.

There were two men in Sheffield I was immensely pleased to have known. One was Bill Owen and the other was George Caborn. Both of them took a liking to me and I felt quite privileged by that. Both of them would ring me at the Poly or at home and ask me if I'd do something because 'the Russians were coming to town' and would I help entertain them, or could I be available for doing this benefit for some union or other. Bill was always interested in my music career. I would often do benefits in the city for 'Hands Off Our Town Hall' and other causes and Bill knew about that. He seemed to know what I was doing. It was he and his friends who would say 'Ask Roy to come and do it' and whenever I could I would.

Bill used to delight in all sorts of things. I would drive him home from the Northern College from time to time and he was always telling me a new way to go. I would just come down through the A61 and into Sheffield and past Hillsborough. Never drove himself, he would say 'No go up here' and I didn't know where I was, and suddenly we'd turn up the back streets and come out somewhere in Stannington, missing all the central traffic. I'd say I don't know where I'm going. 'Trust me' he'd say, 'trust me'.

There's a road called Rivelin Road which runs down from where he lived on Rangeley Road down to Rivelin Valley Road. It's a bendy steep hill and I remember driving down there one day and he said 'See those railings?' - banister metal railings all the way down by the curb which you could hold onto. He said he had helped to put them there because old people walking down the road used to slip in the winter. When he talked about these things, it wasn't about being chairman of the Sheffield City Polytechnic governing body or the chair of this that or the other. He just used to be pleased about little things which weren't little things at all in the lives of ordinary people.

I think Bill was an incredibly decent, honest man who was genuinely motivated by a commitment to others. I don't want to sound sycophantic, but I never heard him say anything ungenerous about anybody. He would say ungenerous things about class, about how he saw the world in terms of the class system, but he never attacked anybody personally.

The Northern College is a testament to Bill's commitment, because if you look at its history in the wider history of the economics of the time it's arguable that the college shouldn't have survived. There were cutbacks everywhere in its early days and the Labour government of the time was doing its share of cutting. Throughout the 80s, when there were assaults and attacks on local authorities from the Conservatives, it was Bill whose persistent voice both in Sheffield and in South Yorkshire made a major contribution to the Northern College's survival. **99**

Bob Fryer succeeded Michael Barratt Brown as principal of the Northern College in August 1983. He had been Chair of the Faculty of Social Studies at the University of Warwick and head of its sociology department. He was also involved in the University's establishment of its own continuing education department, previously under the auspices of Birmingham University's extramural department.

Bob Fryer

"Bill had three or four powerful qualities and these were extremely important for the college. He had a very clear vision of the purpose of the college and its educational functions - who were supposed to be its main beneficiaries, what its educational programme should be. This vision was always in his mind when he was making decisions. We were there to serve the educational needs and interests of people who hadn't had much of a first chance - people who were educationally, socially, economically and racially disadvantaged, or disadvantaged by virtue of being a woman. He felt that the driving force in any policy decision we made, in any appointment we made, was 'How does this help to achieve our objectives?' That was always in his mind.

Secondly he felt that the college should be an outlet for people who worked in and served their communities. He saw it very much as being an outgrowth of voluntary, community activity of one kind or another, which he exemplified in his own life. That community and voluntary activity could be formal, through a trade union, or it could be through a community group, a group of parents, a group of women, or a tenants' association. He was very strong on the college being a resource for volunteers in their communities, and he could see the huge advantage to a city like Sheffield of such a resource.

Another thing which he always had very clearly in his mind was that the college was based on a partnership - first of all expressed between the four South Yorkshire authorities. It wasn't a question of one authority trying to outflank or dominate or hold back the other authorities, although characteristically Bill teased other authorities about their policies. They were partners in the project and therefore they should work together.

But it was also a partnership between the staff of the college and the governing body of the college. I can never in the whole ten years I worked closely with Bill remember him wanting to set up any kind of a division or a conflict between the employees and the staff of the college who were there to serve its purpose, and the governing body. He wasn't one for coming the heavy stick of the governors. He knew where the governors stood, he knew it was a responsibility of the governors to make sure the college stuck to its vision and stuck to its task and did it with efficiency. But he saw the staff and employees of the college as part of that partnership at all times.

The third partnership as far as he was concerned was with the community. He believed the community deserved the best in educational provision that an adult residential college could provide. He always strove to make sure that the interests of all parties to the partnership were reflected in the college's decisions. It's what gave Bill a remarkably clear set of criteria for making decisions.

How did he do it? With a lovely quiet humour, an unpretentious personal style, a very quiet style. Very often he would - what they say in South Yorkshire - 'cod' people. He would kid them and tease them with a twinkle and an amusing approach that was used as a mask for a much more serious intent underneath. He would tease them about an opinion or a position that they were putting forward and show that it didn't square with the kind of vision and commitment I've talked about earlier. His personal style was to be careful, to be thoughtful, to be courteous to people.

When he was in the chair or was vice-chair I had a very close working relationship with him. He would ask me to go and see him to talk through policies, or proposals, or the budget, or whatever happened to be the issue of the day, and in close personal contact like that he was never any different. No side to this man at all. Here was a man who was deeply steeped in the values of the Labour movement and spoke with the authority of the city council and yet showed no side in his personal relationships with someone like me, who was a very young principal when I first came - a few weeks off my 39th birthday.

It's true now, but it was even truer then, that some elements in the British

Labour movement - men in particular - tend to be a bit macho in their personal styles, tend to throw their weight about a bit. That wasn't Bill's style. I can't think of anybody who exemplified better a careful, courteous, humorous, sensitive approach, but he did it all within the framework of having a clear vision of what we should stand for and what our duties and responsibilities were to the community that financed us and supported us. I always found that very, very attractive.

He was also one of the most generous men you could hope to meet, and that generosity manifested itself in lots of ways. He was very generous with his own property. He gave extremely valuable books and collections of books and articles to the Northern College library so that the kind of students he thought the college was there to serve could benefit from them.

But his generosity also showed itself to interviewees when he chaired or was a member of interview panels. Being interviewed for a job is one of the worst things that can happen to you, and he was extremely generous to candidates for jobs. He was also extremely sharp in knowing who would be a good appointment and who wouldn't. Many a person who didn't even know who Bill was must have come away with a favourable impression of a personal style which was enquiring and thoughtful but was also fairly helpful.

The Northern College owes a lot of its existence to Bill, and he never lost faith with the college and what it stood for. When we were seeking funds to start developing the Home Farm site as a residential facility for the students, Bill helped persuade the Transport and General Workers to give us a low interest loan.

Something is happening now that came too late for Bill. For a long time he felt that as the college expanded and offered a more diverse educational programme it needed to strengthen its administrative structures, and he always argued that we needed what he used to call a chief administrative officer - it was one of his campaigns. We almost got there once but a lack of funds and resources prevented us from actually agreeing it, except in principle. For the first time this year we will now have such a post. It will be called assistant principal (administration) but it's the post that Bill always argued that we needed.

Obviously as he got more frail he needed help, but even when he was extremely ill he would still make the journey out to the Northern College. Increasingly he had to be assisted to get there for meetings, but it was always evident that members of staff, whether employees of Sheffield City Council or of the college, would be only too willing to give him a lift in or drop him off at home. So loved was he that people never saw this as a duty but as a great pleasure, a chance to talk to him, and to listen to his wonderful stories about early days in the Labour Party and the politics and history of Sheffield and adult education. **”**

Action Man Mayor ....

Off-beat successes for

Councillor Owen .... Lord

Mayor in political rumpus

.... Champion of the hikers

.... Bill's 50 years of hard

work and caring . . . .

C H A P T E R   F O U R T E E N
Press Relations

Throughout his elder statesman years, Bill Owen had a reasonably good press. By the time he became Lord Mayor in 1980, his days of trade union confrontation with management, bailing out colleagues and friends arrested on picket lines, and defending shop stewards from virulent, often inaccurate, attacks in local newspapers, were over. His time in the public eye was now spent representing the city of Sheffield, receiving its Freedom, and being honoured by the Polytechnic he had helped to create and expand. He was still deeply involved in committees and boards running further and adult education establishments, but these were seldom the stuff of banner headlines.

Making his acceptance speech on the day he received Freedom of the City of Sheffield in 1991, with Lord Mayor, Mrs Dorothy Askham, in the chair

Local reporters found that he became more approachable as he grew older, but he could still not come to terms with the catchy quote or the slick soundbite. And although he began to relax his guard with a younger generation of journalists he recognised were more sympathetic to his ideas than their predecessors in the press of the 1920s, 30s and 40s, he could not, or would not, use them for personal or party advantage.

The two principal local newspapers, the Sheffield Telegraph (later renamed the Morning Telegraph) and The Star, were reasonably fair and balanced in their news coverage of local politics, leaving partisan comment to the editorial columns. Even the leader writers were ready to recognise the important contributions of the left-wingers - and not only when they were safely dead.

Peter Harvey was municipal correspondent of the Sheffield Morning Telegraph for nearly a decade in the 1960s. He later became features editor of the paper before launching his celebrated humorous column more than 21 years ago. The column survived the closure of the Telegraph in 1986, transferring to The Star, where it still appears regularly.

As the Telegraph's chief source of local government news, Peter Harvey spent long hours at the town hall before government legislation opened committees up to the press, lobbying chairmen and opposition spokesmen, and talking with maverick elements who might be ready to leak information the ruling Labour Group hugged to itself. His job brought him close to most of the leading figures in the council though less so to Bill Owen, who chaired none of the major committees such as town planning, finance, housing or general purposes, and who never saw himself as a spokesman for education.

" You couldn't help getting close to these people. While I was doing that job I was probably closer to people working in the town hall and members of the city council than I was to people in the office. I think some of my colleagues felt that that was bad, that you were in some way diluting your credibility as a journalist if you were always giving the town hall's point of view. That wasn't the case. Before you could do that job you had to

Peter Harvey

understand what it was about, and you could only do that by close contact, getting to know what made them tick.

More than anything it took trust, and I was struggling for the first six months. I had known Ron Ironmonger since I was a kid and didn't really have any trouble with him. But when you have committee chairmen saying 'Oh, it's a young feller', you know you have to work at it before they come across with the information. Some were worse than others, some were pretty good. But I was lucky that that was a time when people like Roy Hattersley and George Sharpe and Chris Price were coming in, and they were younger men for a start. Before that you had to be on the council for about thirty years before you got a deputy chairmanship. Then suddenly you had people like Roy Hattersley becoming a deputy chairman and Chris Price becoming deputy on education with Alderman Ballard. In a sense they were professional people, and we hadn't had too many of them in the Labour Group.

The older city fathers were forces to be reckoned with, of course. Labour Group policy and Labour Group decisions were virtually determined by about seven or eight people. When the group officers approved something they recommended it to the executive where they had a majority. And when the executive recommended it to the full group they'd debate it, maybe make some changes - there were probably cases where things were taken back if the group didn't like them - but more often than not whatever that small handful of people had decided went through.

Roy Hattersley helped open things up for the press but he wasn't on his own. There were other people like Price and Sharpe and later on Peter Jones. They didn't have the background that the older people did - believing the press was always against them - and they were more aware of the value of getting their ideas over in the paper. The sad thing in 1968, when the Tories took over, was to see the total chaos in the Labour Group. They didn't know how to handle opposition, and only a couple of weeks after the Tories took control, Ron Ironmonger came out with a diatribe against the press, saying they were totally ignoring what the Labour Group were doing. I did a piece in the Telegraph because I was a bit niggled by this.

The truth was that when you approached the Conservatives, they'd been in opposition so long they knew how to handle it. They would come out of a meeting and say 'We're going to fight this one,' or 'We've moved an amendment.' When the Labour Group were in opposition, I'd go to the Tory chairman and ask what happened and he'd tell me, but the Labour man would say he knew nothing. None of them were saying anything. In the feature, I listed the times and people I'd spoken to - one was Bill Owen - when they had moved an amendment to the Tory proposals and not told me about it.

The Labour Group didn't know how to oppose because they'd been in power for so long. I don't think there was any Labour member of that council who'd ever been in opposition. And for someone like Bill Owen it was more difficult still because he wasn't a forthcoming man. Once Ron Ironmonger realised what was happening he set about putting things right - when you come out of the committee meeting you see the press, you tell them what you've been doing, he must have said. You tell them what was wrong with what the Tories were doing, you don't walk past and say 'No, it's up to him, see him,' because that won't do. But Bill was not the sort of bloke who found that easy to do, because he wasn't a natural communicator with the press. He'd stop and have a little jest with you, he was good with his witticisms, but he wasn't very good at telling you what had happened in the committee.

Opposition for a year shook the Labour councillors out of their complacency - because they'd had the attitude that they were fireproof, impervious. And let's face it, had it not been for special circumstances of boundary changes which meant all council seats were up for re-election instead of one in three they would have been. Under normal election procedures it would have taken three years to get them out because of their large majority. The main cause of their defeat was the rent rebate scheme but that on its own wouldn't have done it. The sudden realisation that they could lose Sheffield shook them up. There were committee chairmen I saw in tears.

The Labour Group made mistakes, of course, and those mistakes attracted wide publicity. But you have to set them in context, and you have to set Bill Owen's time on the council and Ron Ironmonger and all the rest of them in context. They were in the driving seat at a time when suddenly everything was possible, when things they had been waiting 30 years for could suddenly be done.

People tend to think that when the war ended in 1945 everything went back to normal, and it didn't. From 1945 up to 1950 they could do nothing. There were still masses of restrictions, shortages of labour and materials. In 1947 there was the Big Freeze and that messed things up as well with the shortage of coal another problem. It wasn't until the late 1950s - fifteen years after the end of the war - that suddenly things became available and became possible, and over the next ten to fifteen years everything was done in a hell of a rush.

The trouble was the council didn't always get the best advice. Nobody in national government - whichever party was in power - told them there was going to be a sudden explosion of car ownership. So they were basing all their road building on a small annual increase in cars and then people started buying cars and you had them in droves.

The council assumed you had to build masses of houses because there were enormous waiting lists for houses and people couldn't find anywhere to live. To some extent this was true, but it wasn't as bad as it appeared to be. The council couldn't extend the boundaries so they hadn't the land to build Parson Cross and Southey all over again, or even Arbourthorne and the Manor. A delegation went to the Continent and they came back and said 'They're building flats, tall flats, building them fast.' So that's what happened in Sheffield. At the same time the government decided factory building was the thing. Instead of being affected by the weather you build all your components indoors in a factory. And of course that didn't work out either.

Councillors like Bill Owen, who had their roots in the 20s and 30s, were adaptable by and large and entered wholeheartedly into this rush to get things done. They had been frustrated, and now they were keen to get on with it. They had to be adaptable, they'd no choice really, and in a sense perhaps they were too adaptable. If they had slowed down a bit, and taken more time to think, they might not have done some of the things they did.

But I don't want to suggest they made a lot of cock-ups. They made a few, and even despite those, the councillors of that generation are still remembered with respect and are still held in high regard. A lot of the things they did were tremendous, and were supported by everyone in the city. The clean air campaign was a good example. It was followed through from beginning to end with total commitment, and even during their one year of rule the Conservatives didn't make a single change in that. They changed a hell of a lot, but they didn't change the clean air policy. **"**

Mark Pickering joined the Sheffield Morning Telegraph in 1968 as municipal reporter, working closely with Peter Harvey and succeeding him as municipal correspondent in 1970. He was the paper's labour correspondent for 18 months, and for two years was a National Union of Journalists delegate to Sheffield Trades and Labour Council, before leaving to become press officer of Kirklees metropolitan council in 1975. He has now set up his own public relations company in Sheffield.

"I remember canvassing in Darnall for Bill Owen in the 1969 election, when I had been in Sheffield for only a few months. The editor at the time, Michael Finley, called me in and tore me off a strip for getting personally involved that way - and quite rightly so, of course. But Bill Owen was the sort of person you were ready to work for.

Mark Pickering

His own workload must have been phenomenal if you count just the number of colleges and organisations he was responsible for. Apart from anything else, there were a hell of a lot of meetings to attend. But he was involved in local government at a time when it was hard work but positive work. It must have been rewarding for all those councillors who could see they were improving their city, whether it was building a new reservoir or a new school, or clearing the slums from Netherthorpe - whatever they were doing, it was something positive. The council today is little more than a fire-fighting exercise by comparison.

Bill was definitely wary of journalists until he began to talk to people like myself and Mike Bower and Bob Bennett, and realised that the press was not directly related to Lord Rothermere en masse, and that we were to be trusted. But even then, the idea of actually slipping somebody a line was beyond him. He couldn't bring himself to do it because he wasn't that sort of person, not a wheeler-dealer. He was the reverse of Machiavellian. He could make a case for what he believed in, but not necessarily in a public setting .

Early on, I don't think he quite regarded NALGO and the public service unions and the National Union of Journalists as serious unions - we were lucky to be in the same room as the AEU and the T & G chaps who really knew what things were about. But he began to realise that white collar didn't mean automatically dilettante. Although he obviously came from a very traditional manual trade union background, he came to recognise that there were white collar unions with a contribution to make, that had the same views as his, and should not be disregarded or considered to be inferior or unequal in some way. Just as there were manual trade unionists who were probably poorer trade unionists by his criteria than some of the white collar people he came across. He had a flexible mind.

At first sight he didn't have a prepossessing appearance. He was a short man and his hands and feet seemed too big for him. He would never be an elegant figure, and it was easy to be dismissive of him because of that. But that was a very false impression. Looking at him, and knowing his background, you might have been surprised that he could take on board new ideas in quite a flexible way. There were a lot of trade unionists about who thought that if you didn't get your hands grubby you weren't worth talking to. Bill was much larger than that. He was able to grasp the essentials that many others in his generation could not.

I always found him pleasant, extremely pleasant, but I didn't know him well enough to talk about personal matters. I would often pop into his office, either to see him or his organisers, when I was labour correspondent. It was the nearest union to Hartshead, and it was a big union. But I don't feel I ended up knowing him any better. You felt you knew him well, but when you sat down, and had to write what you knew about him, you were never so sure. He was a very quirky man, unconventional. But he never made a fool of himself.

He had power and influence, but you couldn't tell where the power was or where the influence was. When the trades and labour council had to tell the Labour Group what it ought to do, it must have been a difficult exercise. And this is where people like Bill Owen, who was both trades and labour president and a city councillor, came in. He would have been able to convey the message very, very quietly. And I think they must have listened, particularly after they lost power for that one year.

It must have taken influence to be able to go to the Labour Group when they'd just lost control, and say I think you ought to listen to me, I'm president of the trades and labour council and we've got something to tell you. You're in opposition for the first time for forty years, and I think you might be interested in listening to me. He must have had a phenomenally powerful voice. He must have had people listening to him very, very carefully. He was in a unique position at that time.

There was a great deal of delegated power to chairmen in those days, of course, and that was probably undemocratic. But Bill Owen was also an employer, with a level of responsibility in his job which a lot of other Labour councillors wouldn't have had. Bill had staff, he had a building he was responsible for, he had a budget. Many councillors came from the shop floor and would have had responsibility as shop stewards and convenors but not managerial responsibility.

Yet he was frequently under-estimated by people who didn't know him. And people who read this book will under-estimate him, and will not believe that he had that sort of influence, because they don't understand how things are achieved in politics, often behind the scenes, by making a case privately. That's how it happened in those days, more so than it does now when you're not likely to succeed if you don't make a strong case and get some public groundswell behind you .

In Bill's day, the major influence was seen and felt behind doors and in quiet corridors. If you could persuade people like Ron Ironmonger and Izzy Lewis and get them on your side, then your scheme had a chance. Isidore Lewis was finance chairman and had a contingency fund of £1 million - which sounds little these days but was a lot of money then - and Ron Ironmonger was leader and everybody bloody well knew it. If you couldn't get their backing you had no chance. You needed to make a case to them. You wouldn't win by making your case through the newspapers and then hoping they were going to back you.

It was all very well to bang the drum when you had got the scheme through, when you'd talked it out and got council approval. You could bang the drum then and get some publicity. But you made a fundamental mistake if you tried to get people to support you through a bit of coverage in The Star.

And people like Bill knew if a scheme had a chance. Somebody told me once that if Izzy Lewis started polishing his glasses, you'd just lost. He wasn't going to let you have a little bit of his contingency fund. You hadn't made your case properly, and he was about to let you down gently. Your pet scheme had not won his favour.

Ron Ironmonger was a classic big city leader, and a nice man as well. I saw a great deal of him, and we fell out occasionally when I asked questions he didn't want to answer, or when he thought I was being a bit presumptuous. He would tell me off, and you felt told off when he was the one doing it! When he was knighted, he insisted on being Sir Ron, not Sir Ronald. I remember interviewing him the day before he was knighted and he said 'Well, it's nice for me, because I'm going to be Sir Ron. But my wife's always been a lady, so it won't make any difference to her.' That was a nice thing to say. **"**

Bob Bennett was education correspondent of the Sheffield Morning Telegraph from 1968 to 1977. He worked as a news reporter and a general feature writer, and became the newspaper's features editor before leaving in 1985 to join Sheffield education department as press officer.

" One of the things I admired about Bill Owen was that his commitment to training was total and that was typical of him. There wasn't much media coverage in training, no real glamour, and few people who were not directly involved really understood it. But he continued to champion it. He was a tremendously hard worker, probably because he felt there was so much to be achieved. There was a strong feeling about at the time that the Labour movement was changing Sheffield for the better, building something new that would be better for them and better for Sheffield people.

Bob Bennett

He worked long hours. I remember saying goodnight to him on the way home at about 11.30 at night, and then seeing him go past the Telegraph offices to Transport House first thing in the morning. I'm sure there is still that level of commitment in the Labour movement but they're on the defensive all the time, so the sense of optimism and purpose that Bill had isn't so evident.

I always felt Bill liked me, but he never showed it. He certainly didn't give me any special news stories, partly because that just wasn't his way of doing things, partly because he didn't want to see his name all over the papers. He was very diffident about personal publicity. But I always enjoyed meeting him. He was good company and always entertaining - almost a working class version of the upper class eccentric.

He was a self-effacing man who made very few speeches, at least in public, yet he exerted so much influence over a long period. I could never fully understand how such a self-effacing man could end up as district secretary of the TGWU - one of the most powerful and certainly the biggest trade union in the area - and manage it so well.

But then he wasn't above sorting people out. I saw him lose his temper at trades council quite often, although it would be more accurate to say that he was exasperated rather than angry. It was exasperation with members' reluctance to do what he was telling them to do, and exasperation with their naivety as well. It was usually aimed at white collar unions like NALGO, as if he was trying to tell them 'You're in a room of real trade unionists now.'

I am sure he had a vision. That's a modern word, and perhaps he wouldn't understand what was meant by it, but I believe he saw further education in visionary terms - as a more effective avenue for working class progress than the academic route.

He was a big supporter of the youth service and that has always been a highly unpopular section of the service. People have seldom understood what it's about, and George Wilson actually tried to close parts of it down when he was Labour group leader. But Bill always fought for it. The youth service, adult education and further education were all major interests - and they were all about helping working class kids he believed the school system had failed. Bill championed them when they were very unglamorous, minority interests, and he supported them through some very unpopular and quite public incidents.

The Bow Centre was set up to stop unemployed kids hanging round the city centre with nowhere to go, nothing to do. It was Bill who lent his weight to the idea of bringing them in to interest them in something worthwhile. He was never solely interested in those areas of education which were 'safe and boring.' He backed a centre for truants and that was set up unofficially - I don't think it went to any committee. Headteachers were very upset about it at the time, but Bill continued to back it, and that took a lot of doing. Bill showed obstinacy and determination, because it wasn't a popular issue. It was a remarkable thing to do at that time because truancy was seen as just a disciplinary issue. Offering truants an alternative to school was a real challenge to the education establishment but he took that on.

It says a lot about his integrity that he would support issues even when he could see they had a potential for attracting trouble. If he saw the sense in something he followed it through, whatever people thought. He was never content simply to go along with the establishment and he was never slow to speak out when he thought they should be going along with him.

I think his willingness to support projects which were unglamorous or even dangerous came from a faith in ordinary people and an enormous tolerance for people's failings. I'm sure he believed that everyone has it in them to do well if they get the right chance at the right time, and I think his work in education was about giving them that chance.

His trust in people came home to me when the journalists of the Telegraph and Star were locked out. Journalists are such an odd bunch at the best of times, yet he opened up Transport House for us and gave us the freedom of the building, knowing that some of us had spent our working lives attacking trade unions and the city council whatever they did. The scene in the assembly hall was chaotic most of the time, with some people playing bridge non-stop, others sleeping off lunchtime drink - all sorts. Bill just smiled to himself the way he did and let us get on with it. **"**

CHAPTER FIFTEEN
The Action Man Mayor

O ne of the more idiosyncratic sights that residents of the select Whirlow Lane area of Sheffield still recall from 1980 and 1981 is of a slightly built, silver-haired man wearing a mayoral chain and walking a poodle. Bill Owen had his own priorities, even as the 84th Lord Mayor of the city, and one of them was his love for animals. An official limousine may have been en route to whisk him from the official residence at Whirlow Court to another official engagement, but dog walking could not be missed. And he showed no embarrassment when the poodle, shut in a bedroom to prevent its getting under the feet of distinguished dinner guests, left a solid protest on the cream-coloured carpet.

With dozens of visits, lunches and dinners scheduled every week, however, Bill Owen was more than merely conscientious as Sheffield's first citizen, failing to turn up for only one engagement - his first. A Dutch tourist promotion dinner at the Cutlers' Hall had been entered in his diary for a week later. He enjoyed being Lord Mayor, and he enjoyed using Whirlow Court, partly because it gave him and his wife Sheila a chance to relax in their brief off-duty hours.

"He wasn't sure about being Lord Mayor at first. I think he would have liked to have been chosen maybe two or three years later. He always said that when Lord Mayors went back to the council they had lost all their positions, and he didn't want that. But when he got into it he was very happy and he enjoyed it," Sheila Owen recalls.

"He didn't like the dressing up either, but then he realised he'd got to do it. The Lord Mayor's secretary, Colin Straw, told us what we must buy in the way

Making the most of a press photo opportunity

Lord and Lady Mayoress

of clothes, and Bill said 'Oh dear, all those suits,' and I said 'If you need them, you need them.' When he had to buy his pinstripe trousers and his black jacket he said 'I can't imagine myself in them,' but he did look smart, and they suited him, especially with his white hair.

"Bill liked being at Whirlow and he was upset when they stopped using it as the residence for the Lord Mayor. It was very handy to pop back just for a few minutes to relax, and not have to think you've got to do housework. I don't know how we'd have managed without it, because it would have been impossible to run a home as well. There were a lot of staff up there and they were all very kind. They didn't mind what they had to do for you, and if they had to work a bit over they never worried."

There were other practical advantages to living in an official residence during their early months in office. On the eve of their installation as Lord and Lady Mayoress on May 21 1980, Sheila's mother suffered a stroke. She died six days later, without regaining consciousness. When her father failed to appear at the ceremony, Sheila believed her mother had already died.

"It was the unhappiest day of my life. I didn't want to ask my family until after the ceremony, and then my sister Jean told me she was still unconscious, but it didn't look as if she would recover and my dad thought it was too much to come to the installation."

After the funeral, her father moved to Sheffield to be with them, but within six months he, too, had suffered a stroke and died - "He loved being at Whirlow Court. They were very good with him. He was a big strong fellow, the last person I thought would have a stroke. But they were very close, my dad and my mum."

The recurring family tragedies could not blight their year in office, however. According to local newspapers it began well, with a strong speech from Bill Owen which centred inevitably on education and on a defence of trade unions. His theme for the year was "Sheffield competes" and the new

Lord Mayor showed his determination to interpret that widely when he launched an Olympics appeal fund to send British athletes to Moscow. Without condoning the Soviet invasion of Afghanistan which had prompted Britain's refusal to send an official team, Bill Owen wrote a letter to The Star in which he urged: "As the athletes have freely decided to take part, the British public should see they are able to do so, free from financial worry and restraint."

He made the headlines again in June 1980 when he criticised plans to cut 500 jobs at the Manpower Services Commission headquarters at Moorfoot in Sheffield. He argued that, with unemployment at a record level, the MSC should be increasing its services rather than cutting back.

Wherever he spoke, his dry humour was usually apparent, but it was not always understood or appreciated. Welcoming Sheffield Wednesday to a town hall reception after they had won promotion to second division football, he told them "There are only two teams in Sheffield - Sheffield Wednesday and Sheffield Wednesday reserves." Unsmiling United officials failed to see the joke, and he was not asked to visit Bramall Lane again.

"It was a joke said because of the occasion, but I don't think the reaction worried him. When Bill was Lord Mayor he always went to the home matches of Wednesday if it was possible, and the crowd used to shout 'Keep coming Lord Mayor, keep coming,' because he never saw them lose. They started to lose when we visited Zambia, but they were way ahead till then," Sheila remembers.

The Lord Mayor and Lady Mayoress had more than enough invitations to occupy them, seldom less than a dozen each week. During Christmas week in 1980 there were more than 30 engagements in their diary, and throughout the year Bill was determined to visit as many schools as he could squeeze in.

"There were so many engagements it was unbelievable. With Bill's trade union links we had to go to London a lot for receptions and dinners. In fact, it was the first time in my life that I have gone to a reception in the evening and not had time to wash. I used to buy Quickies, do my face in the car coming back, and then go straight out. We used to lay out our clothes - or sometimes even take them to the Town Hall - because we knew we wouldn't have time to get ready."

For the Lady Mayoress, one of the personal highlights of the year in office was opening Hathersage Carnival. "They asked me to do it because I came from Hathersage, and Colin Straw didn't want me to, because it was outside our boundary. But Bill said 'If Sheila wants to do it, we'll do it.' And I know everybody in Hathersage was so pleased. It's only a village and they all thought it was marvellous. I really enjoyed that day."

In May 1981, shortly before handing over to their successors, Bill and Sheila travelled to Zambia to forge twinning links between Sheffield and Kitwe. In a busy programme, they met President Kaunda at his palace, and visited the world's largest opencast mine at Chingola and the rain forests at the Victoria Falls. As they travelled the country, they met dozens of ex-patriates.

The local people were hospitable and often overwhelmingly friendly, but

Bill and Sheila visiting the world's largest opencast mine at Chingola in May 1981 during a visit to Zambia to forge links between Sheffield and Kitwe.

Colin Straw, who accompanied the mayoral party, must have been as intrigued as the Owens were by the welcoming notice they saw in Chimwemwe:

The Lord Mayor and the Mayoress as well as the secretary to your cabinet, we as Chimwemwe ward we are giving you a thunderous welcome as the indication of the relationship which is between two cities Kitwe and Sheffield. Hence we are obliged to assure you that the relationship between the two cities of Sheffield and city of Kitwe will be a perpetual one as to encourage human relationship both financially and economically.

"We actually went to talk about the twinning, but really spent more time in schools and down copper mines," Sheila points out. "Bill tried to get some books and pens and other things sent out to them, because they had literally nothing in those schools. It was very, very poor."

Their year in office over, the Owens took a short holiday, visiting Paris, Brussels, and Amsterdam. When they returned to Sheffield, Bill Owen got down to work again, no longer an officer of the Transport and General Workers Union, but still a local councillor in Walkley with countless surgeries, public meetings, committees and boards of governors to attend.

Ten years later, on September 19 1991, there was no limousine waiting to take the Owens to the Town Hall for the ceremony in which Bill Owen would become the 58th Freeman of the City. Instead, they caught a bus from Walkley to the city centre and walked the last few hundred yards. Surprised friends, who would have picked the Owens up in their cars, could only smile and tell themselves "That's Bill ... "

The lifelong trade unionist and politician may have wanted to share only with Sheila his anticipation of receiving one of the few honours he was happy about accepting. He had been offered and refused honours from the Queen, and he had joked with colleagues that OBEs were too often given for "other buggers' efforts". But he was deeply touched by the recognition of his city council colleagues.

CHAPTER SIXTEEN
A Private Life

With Cookie

T here were many friends and colleagues who believed that Bill Owen had little time left over from his union, political and education work for a personal life. If you measured his home life by the number of hours he actually spent there, they would have been right. But the few people with whom he shared a close friendship confirm that Bill knew how to relax, how to enjoy his walks in the country, his books, his music, his rose-growing, his holidays abroad after his second marriage and his frequent drop-in chats with his constituents in Walkley.

A familiar and welcome face at so many meetings and rallies, Bill Owen was a private man as soon as they were over. He loved driving out into the countryside or dining out at good restaurants with his wife Sheila. And during his last 12 years, neighbours always knew he was home when they heard him calling his cat indoors. "Cookie was his favourite. She would come when he called, sit on his knee and put her paws on his shoulders. She didn't eat for ten days after Bill's death," says Sheila. Those quiet moments, and the privacy of his thoughts, must have been a necessary counter-balance in a life which had been constantly driven by other people's needs, other people's problems.

From the day he left the family home in Burnaby Street, Bill Owen's home life was influenced by three women. The day after his room had been damaged in an air raid, he moved in with his sister Bertha and her husband Sid Bingham, who lived in Frecheville. He stayed with them until his first marriage in 1950. His brother-in-law worked shifts as a wire drawer at Firth Brown so Bill fitted in well until the Binghams had children - "Bertha was glad to have someone in the house at nights," said Bill.

He met Joan Calvert through the Holiday Fellowship Club when she still worked in the millinery department at Cockayne's store (it later became

Schofields). They married 12 months later on April 1 1950 at St Giles Church, living in a back-to-back house in Hanover Street for six months before buying a semi-detached house in Den Bank Crescent, Crosspool.

"When her employers knew who she was marrying, they would not employ her any more," Bill told an interviewer nearly 40 years later. "Joan was very loyal to me, but she was very reserved. She was soon snubbed. If she had lived another couple of days, we would have been married 25 years. She was in the Royal Hospital with another complaint and the consultant took me on side and told me she had cancer. I didn't tell her, but when she went to another doctor he blurted it out."

Joan had little interest in politics, though most of their holidays were taken at one conference or another - the Labour Party, the TUC, the TGWU - usually in Bournemouth, Brighton, or Blackpool. Joan would sit in the hotel foyer or walk on the promenade while Bill was mixing with delegates. But she was always there.

When she died in St Luke's nursing home on March 30 1976, Bill was grief-stricken and his friends offered comfort and, when he seemed willing to accept it, practical help. The ward Labour Party chairman and secretary in Walkley, Barry and Dorothy Whittington were specially close to Bill. Dorothy also worked for him at the T & G office as his "permanent temp", filling in if one of the cleaning ladies was ill or on holiday.

"Joan was not very political, but she supported him and agreed with a lot of his policies. She realised that he was dedicated to politics and to Sheffield, and I think she just took a back seat. She kept the home going so that Bill had a base he could always go back to," said Barry.

Shortly after Joan's death, Dorothy asked Bill if she could do any washing for him - "He was always immaculate and had at least one clean shirt on every day" - but he told her he had done the washing himself.

"He said 'No, but I've got some ironing,' so we went round to collect it. It was a yard high and it was absolutely bone dry, and I hate ironing things that are bone dry. So I did that lot and told him I'd do his washing as well because I couldn't stand having to damp everything down. 'Fair enough' he said, so we fetched his washing one Sunday, took it back the next Sunday, and picked another load up.

"Barry began picking him up in the car to bring him back from meetings and they would stop off at Bill's house to turn on the electric blanket before driving to our house for supper. We'd have a chat and try to get him to talk about Joan, so that he wasn't bottling it up. We were always there if he needed us and that's what happened."

Bill spent the Christmas after Joan's death with the Whittingtons and their son John - "He suddenly realised what Christmas was for, and I think that did him a world of good because he saw John opening his presents. It made him realise that life had to go on," said Barry.

Within a few months, Dorothy played a small but important role in Bill's future happiness. Working at Transport House on holiday relief, she would pop out to buy him a sandwich, a baked potato, or fish and chips to eat in his office. Eventually she pointed out "I'm not going to be working here very much longer. Why don't you have lunch at Schofields - and at least you'll have had one hot meal a day."

The Whittingtons heard nothing more until one evening he arrived at their home to tell them he was going to marry a waitress he had met on those daily visits to the same department store where his first wife had worked.

Sheila Keegan was a very different person from Joan, and she "brought Bill out" according to many friends and observers. She had been born in Hathersage and attended a local school. Her father, Cyril Lowe, was the third generation of his family to farm in the area, and her mother, Rosilla, had also worked hard to keep High Leas farm a productive unit. Sheila's first marriage had ended in divorce.

She remembers Bill proposing - or rather suggesting marriage - the night before he left with a city council delegation for a three week visit to America. "He just said 'When I come back, can we get married?' I hadn't gone out with him that much, so I said I'd decide while he was away."

He sent her postcards every day for those three weeks, and when he returned he immediately went out to Hathersage and asked her mother "Has she told you whether we're going to get married or not?" Mrs Lowe replied "Oh I think she'll consent to it", and over tea Bill asked Cyril Lowe "Well, can we get married then?" His future father-in-law said "It's up to you, Bill, but I'll be very happy," and the couple began making plans for their wedding at Sheffield register office, followed by a reception at the Anglers Rest in Bamford. Councillor Peter Horton, chairman of Sheffield education committee, was Bill's best man, and among the guests were the Lord Mayor of Sheffield, Councillor Winifred Golding, and Martin Flannery, the MP for Hillsborough.

"It might surprise some people but Bill was very romantic," Sheila says. "He used to write romantic little words on the cards that he sent from America, quotes from Jim Reeves songs and other things. I said to my mother 'I bet the postman in Hathersage has had a laugh over these.' I don't know what attracted us to each other because we were so different. Bill had asked me out for weeks before I went with him. He asked me to go to the Messiah at the City Hall and I said no. Then just before Christmas he asked me to the pantomime at the Crucible and I said all right. That was our first date - the pantomime!"

After the wedding, Bill and Sheila began to travel more, enjoying two or three holidays abroad each year with friends in Austria or cruising on the QE2. They opened up their home to Spanish students, and were in turn invited to stay with their families in Spain. Bill particularly liked Portugal, Cyprus and Yugoslavia.

Back in Sheffield, they settled into the typical life of a local councillor and his wife. Bill attended innumerable meetings while Sheila tended house and garden and acted as his "unpaid secretary."

"If he was expecting anybody to telephone him during the day he would leave me leaflets and he would say 'Anyone telephones, read out exactly what I've written. If there's any problem tell them to ring after ten o'clock at night.' He used to come home every day about half past five, unless there were council meetings, have his meal and about half past six, quarter to seven, he'd be off again.

"We would have phone calls at twelve o'clock at night from different people, but Bill was better in the evening than in the morning. He didn't like getting up - that was one of his failings. He had his breakfast in bed every morning, because it was the only way he'd get breakfast, and then he'd get up and have a shower. But he could write until one o'clock in the morning and it was no problem to him. When he came home some nights, I would have lists of people who had rung him. Last Christmas there were so many cards from people, a lot them just dropped them through the letterbox, saying thank you for what Bill had done for them."

To relax, Bill would read, or spend a couple of hours in the front garden of their home in Rangeley Road, tending his roses and chatting with local people as they passed. He enjoyed opera, Gilbert and Sullivan, Jim Reeves, and shows at the Crucible Theatre.

"Bill was a very kind husband, and he'd do anything he possibly could for me. But I knew when he was angry with me, I knew by his face when I couldn't have my own way. Most of the time he would let me do just what I wanted, but I could always tell when I wasn't going to get my own way. I used to look at his face, and I'd think 'Be quiet Sheila, you've lost this one.' It was usually if I was spending a lot. He didn't mind me buying clothes and things, that didn't worry him. But if I wanted something new for the house he would say 'What's wrong with what we've got?' Sometimes he'd give way to me, and sometimes not."

Eighteen months before his death, Bill Owen suffered his first heart attack. Shortly before a meeting at his home with Margaret Anderson, the headmistress of Walkley Junior School, he complained of a pain in the chest and arm. He drank a medicinal brandy, and went ahead with the meeting. Within 45 minutes of its finishing he was admitted to the Hallamshire Hospital.

Bill was determined to fight his illness - "If I give up the town hall, I'm finished" he told Sheila - and slowly resumed his regular meetings. He walked around his ward as often as he could, and read books in Walkley library. Sheila drove out into Derbyshire so that he could enjoy afternoon tea in a favourite cafe in Ashford. He was often worried in his last months - but it was more about problems facing Sheffield than his own condition. He worried about schools closures, he worried that the local authority was not getting enough money, and above all he was worried that the Sheffield electorate would turn against the Labour Party. But, apart from swelling in the ankles and knees, he suffered no serious illness until his final heart attack on September 25 1992.

Sheila Owen recalls it vividly. "I woke up at two o'clock and heard water running. I said 'Bill, have you been in the bathroom?' I stood it so long, then I got up, and heard this noise in the pipe - I've heard it since, it must be an air block. When I came back in the bedroom he said to me, 'See, I haven't left the water running, have I?' and those were the last words he said to me.

"I couldn't sleep very well, so about three o'clock I got up and asked Bill if he wanted to go to the toilet while I was up. He didn't answer me, so I picked his hand up and it just dropped. I was really frightened, but he didn't look ill."

She called in a neighbour who had been a funeral director and he told Sheila that Bill was dead. When the doctor arrived he confirmed the neighbour's words.

Bill Owen's funeral at Hutcliffe Wood crematorium was conducted according to Bill's own wishes by David Botley of Owlerton Church, who had been his chaplain when he was Lord Mayor. But it was not until the leader of Sheffield City Council, Mike Bower, gave the eulogy that many mourners realised just how committed and involved Bill had been in the life of Sheffield for over half a century.

"Mike spoke more than David but that was right because Bill wasn't very religious," says Sheila. "He'd go when he had to, if it was part of his duties. And he'd go to the church in Walkley for coffee. But I think that was because he could sit with the people of Walkley and just talk to them."

CHAPTER SEVENTEEN
Last Words

When you have spent months digesting old newspaper cuttings, and tape recorded more than 30 interviews with your subject's colleagues, friends and family, there comes a moment when you ask yourself if you're in danger of getting the whole thing out of proportion.

Did Bill Owen really have that much of a lasting impact on the political and educational life of Sheffield? So many interviewees said he did that you are left in no doubt about it. He certainly helped give our children a better chance of education in the city's further education colleges and at Sheffield Polytechnic, now Sheffield Hallam University.

But did he really touch the lives of ordinary people? My notebooks were filled with the assurances of men and women who knew Bill Owen better than I did, and about half this book was already written.

I was killing a couple of hours before starting yet another interview when any last doubts about the relevance of those testaments of the past finally disappeared.

I had bought a sandwich, walked across Devonshire Green and sat on a bench under a clump of trees to feed myself and the pigeons. In 25 years of working in Sheffield, I had passed the small open park countless times - it's close to my favourite second-hand book and record shop - but I had never stopped there before.

As I walked back across the grass to the road, I saw a stone plinth topped by a plaque which read:

DEVONSHIRE GREEN
THIS OPEN SPACE IS DEDICATED TO THE MEMORY
OF THOSE CITIZENS OF SHEFFIELD
WHO DIED ON THE NIGHTS OF THE
12TH, 13TH AND 15TH DECEMBER 1940
DURING AERIAL BOMBARDMENT OF THE CITY
IN THE SECOND WORLD WAR 1939-45.

THIS STAND OF FIVE TREES WAS PLANTED BY
THE LORD MAYOR OF SHEFFIELD
(COUNCILLOR W OWEN, JP)
ON THE 14TH DECEMBER 1980
TO COMMEMORATE THE 40TH ANNIVERSARY
OF THE RAIDS.

There are other trees planted by Bill Owen in Sheffield - in a corner of the Peace Gardens close to the town hall, and outside Walkley junior school. There are railings up and down the hills of Walkley which he convinced the works department were a necessary aid for elderly people, particularly in the icy conditions of winter.

His contribution to further and higher education may be commemorated in the Bill Owen building at Sheffield Hallam University and in the library of Northern College, but his achievements were not all on the grand scale. Sheffielders will still exercise their dogs or picnic in the parks from which he removed "Don't walk on the grass" signs. They will still sit and feed pigeons in the shade of trees he planted.

Doubts about Bill Owen's lasting impact on his city disappear when you talk with Members of Parliament who use the word "love" when they recall him, with journalists whose cynicism evaporates as they remember their contacts with him, and with a university administrator who can be moved to tears when she reads a council leader's tribute to a man she knew only in his later years.

Consider these opinions from colleagues:

"Bill was a great motivator" - Richard Caborn

"He was a power behind the scenes" - Peter Horton

"He was one of the last politicians in this city who had his head and his heart in socialism" - Jack Hall

"He had a tremendous gift of mastering the brief" - George Tolley

"Bill was an incredibly decent, honest man ... an unreconstructed socialist" - Roy Bailey

"The great thing about Bill was trust" - John Stoddart

"The Northern College owes a lot of its existence to Bill" - Bob Fryer

"He was frequently underestimated by people who didn't know him" - Mark Pickering

"Not many people are truly good, certainly not in politics, and he was" - Patience Sheard

His family and constituents in Walkley will remember him and assess his influence on their lives in their own way. Three months after Bill's death, Sheila Owen received a letter from his nephew, Bryn Owen, who was a manager in industry before becoming a lecturer at Salford University College and then a management consultant.

"As a child," he wrote, "I remember that he never missed sending us presents at Christmas and these were always books, good books which I am sure he chose with care to help develop in all of us a love for literature. When he met us later in the year he remembered the books and talked to us about them. Although he had no children of his own he clearly loved children and made time to treat them as adults and to listen to them. The high level of educational standards achieved by his nieces and nephews must reflect on the emphasis he and his siblings placed on education.

"One of my proudest moments was when Hugh Scanlon, then Lord Scanlon, visited my factory and I was able to tell him that I was Bill's nephew. We talked of Bill, who was Lord Mayor, and it was clear that he held him in great respect. Bill is someone of whom I am truly proud to say he was my uncle. He demonstrated that through serving his fellow man you can achieve respect and greatness. He came from the humblest of backgrounds but became, through service and dedication, a prince among his equals. It was a privilege to know him."

APPENDIX ONE
A Public Life
(1914-1992)

1936-1992	Member of Transport and General Workers Union 9/236 branch
1945-1980	District officer, then district secretary, of TGWU
1958-1992	Justice of the Peace
1958-1970	Labour Councillor for Darnall
1970-1972	Alderman of the City of Sheffield
1972-1992	Labour Councillor for Walkley
1960-1973	President of Sheffield Trades and Labour Council
1973-1984	President of Sheffield Trades Council
1973-1980	Chairman of Sheffield District Labour Party
1974-1984	President of South Yorkshire Association of Trades Councils
1960-1981	District secretary of Sheffield No 28 district committee of Confederation of Shipbuilding and Engineering Unions
1960-1981	Chairman of trade union side of joint negotiating committee for private sector of steel industry
1965-1980	Chairman of Sheffield and Rotherham district committee of Manpower Services Commission
1980-1981	Lord Mayor of Sheffield
1991	Freeman of the City of Sheffield

Education Activities:

1960-1981	TGWU representative on TUC education advisory committee - Workers' Educational Association
1969-1980	Deputy chairman of Sheffield education committee
1970-1975	Deputy chairman of Sheffield City Polytechnic
1975-1990	Chairman of Sheffield City Polytechnic

1990-1992	Deputy chairman of Sheffield City Polytechnic
1964-1990	Chairman of Granville College of Further Education
1967-1990	Chairman of Shirecliffe College of Further Education
1966-1967	Chairman of Stannington College of Further Education
1975-1992	Sheffield LEA representative on Northern College - chairman and deputy chairman on rota basis
1972-1975	Governor of Myers Grove comprehensive school
1972-1974	Chairman of King Edward VII school
1970-1989	Chairman of Walkley Infants school
1970-1992	Chairman of Walkley Junior school
1975-1990	Chairman of Rivelin First and Middle schools
1989-1992	Governor of Loxley College

Founder member of the Ramblers' Association

APPENDIX TWO

Freeman of the City
Acceptance Speech

Offering me the 58th Freeman of Sheffield is a great honour and is much appreciated. I ask myself what I have done to deserve this honour after 38 years on Sheffield City Council, and I can only assume it is due to my fight for animal rights, moved resolutions, seconded by ex-Councillor Pat Davey, against hare coursing, badger baiting, fox hunting, indiscriminate slaughter of whales and seals, the banning of circuses with wild animals performing in public parks - all carried with overwhelming majorities.

Secondly there is adult education, with which I have been actively involved the whole of my 38 years on the council. May I remind you that Sheffield pioneered adult education, the first general secretary of the WEA being Ernest Green, a steelworker from Samuel Fox of Stocksbridge. In 1919 the Plebs League was founded by Frank Horrobin in Springvale road, along with the monthly journal Plebs, which became the organ of the National Council of Labour Colleges which succeeded the Plebs League.

Also in 1919, the Sheffield Educational Settlement was opened at Shipton Street, Upperthorpe, by Arnold Freeman, one of three sons of Sidney Freeman, founder of the Manikin cigars company. The other two sons were Peter, a Labour MP for Newport, and Ralph, the designer and architect of Sydney Harbour, Australia. Both institutions were in what is now Netherthorpe ward.

Many of the past fathers of this council were students at the Sheffield Educational Settlement and were in classes which were jointly under the auspices of the WEA and the extra-mural department of Sheffield University. The three most prominent of these were Ernest Rowlinson, the leader of the Labour Party when Labour came to power in 1926, along with Frank Thraves and Albert Ballard.

In 1969, when Labour regained power after one year out of office the late Ron Ironmonger, chief whip of the then Labour Group, asked me if I would accept deputy chair of education to be anchorman to Peter Horton, who was to be chair.

Michael Harrison had been appointed chief education officer, with John Mann his deputy and Brian Hanson the senior assistant education officer responsible for further and higher education, and the council was moving from the grammar school system to comprehensive education, so we had the task of setting up the instruments and articles of the four colleges of further education, Granville, Richmond, Shirecliffe and Stannington. This paved the way for the new College of Technology in Pond Street to be redesignated as one of the first three polytechnics and I had the privilege of being chair of governors of the Polytechnic from 1974 to 1990, working with two principals, George Tolley and John Stoddart.

Peter Horton and I then had the task of drawing up the instruments and articles for school governors which came into being in the early seventies, and of course the Labour Group took the initiative for founding Northern College at Wentworth Castle for second chance students, including many women.

I have said little about my trade union activities. I have been district secretary of the Transport and General Workers Union, district secretary of the Confederation of Shipbuilding and Engineering Unions, president of the trades and labour council and the District Labour Party.

I have been fortunate in gaining a wide experience which has held me in good stead as a Sheffield city councillor.

Bill Owen, September 19 1991

Acknowledgements

A tribute to Bill Owen might have been written without the help and encouragement of the following, but it's doubtful:

Sheila Owen, Bryn Owen

Councillors Doris Askham, Mike Bower, Jean Cromar, Peter Horton, Bill Jordan, Doris Mulhearn and ex-councillors Pat Davey (Santhouse), Winifred Golding, Reg Munn, Patience Sheard.

Roy Bailey, Albert Bedford, Michael Barratt Brown, Richard Caborn, Tony Davis, Keith Farnsworth, Blanche Flannery, Martin Flannery, Bob Fryer, Sylvia Greenwood, Jack Hall, Michael Harrison, Jack Illingworth, Lillian Munn, Peter Newman, John Stoddart, Vernon Thornes, Dr George Tolley, Eric Wardle, Heide Wiedemann, Barry Whittington, Dorothy Whittington.

Rob Harrison, Sally Neocosmos, Maggi White.

Sheffield Newspapers, who permitted free access to their photographic library.

Special thanks to Bob Bennett, Peter Harvey and Mark Pickering for their editorial guidance, and to Elizabeth Holloway who transcribed more than 30 taped interviews with no more than the anticipated (and justified) number of complaints.

July 1993

Portraits of a City Father